Hoo's Who

A century of memories

by

Evans and Douglas Marsh

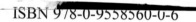
ISBN 978-0-9558560-0-6

Front cover illustration shows: Eastborough Farm, Cooling, Fred
Muggeridge, 2 workers, Edwin Bucknall and a collection of pots
discovered on the farm from an old roman pottery.

Hoo's Who

A century of Memories

Preface

Memory shifts and changes and drifts away when its owners leave us.

Doug Marsh wanted to preserve the memories of his friends from the Hundred of Hoo. He wanted to capture their character and way of life in their own words, to both cherish and share them. Sadly, Doug died before the scrappy manuscript I gave him in hospital, born of his idea, became an actual book.

There is something for everyone in this book, take what you want from it but enjoy meeting these people, as I did. If tractors or corn prices aren't your thing, nod sagely and skip a few pages – they won't mind.

My grateful thanks go to all who contributed, I apologise for spelling mistakes and incorrect names, without Doug to edit for me I was lost. Apologies to those who were interviewed but are not present Joan Chinnery, Cyril and Madge Button, Dee Clarabut and Peta Whitebread (to name a few). I had technical problems with your tapes – sorry.

Thanks to Leah Bradley, Mary Collins and Jeffrey Evans who contributed in different ways to keeping me sane and helping me finish.

Finally, my huge and heartfelt thanks go to Sue, Doug's wife, for giving him up so often in pursuit of this project. I hope he has found an Angelic Fenn Bell and is laughing now, at some tale told by his cousin Arthur or his dear friend Dr. Chris Rigby. It's a great privilege to have him as my sons Godfather; I know Doug will always watch over Archie.

Kathy

Index

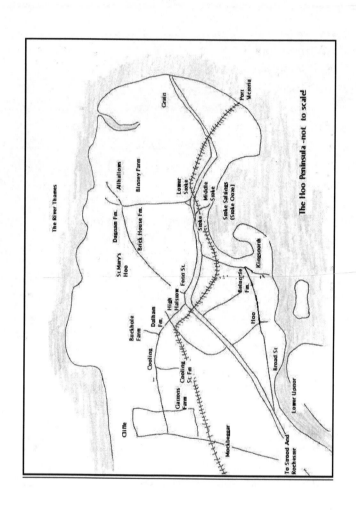

The Hoo Peninsula –not to scale!

The River Thames

Cliffe

Buckhole Farm

Gattons Farm

Cooling

Cooling St. Fm

Mockbeggar

St. Mary's Hoo

Dalham Fm.

High Halstow

Fenn St.

Dagnam Fm.

Brick House Fm.

Allhallows

Binney Farm

Grain

Lower Stoke

Stoke

Middle Stoke

Stoke Saltings
(Stoke Ooze)

Kingsnorth

Beluncle Fm.

Hoo

Broad St

Lower Upnor

Port Victoria

To Strood And Rochester

6

Doug Marsh

Doug, his father and daughter Elizabeth

I was born in 12 St Mary's Cottages in 1927 and brought up in St. Mary's Hoo. My father was in partnership there with a man called Harry Smith. We moved to High Halstow when I was quite young – I spent an awful lot of time at Buckhole Farm - that was my aunt's.

I lived with my Aunt for quite a bit, for various reasons. I was very happy there. I was happier at Buckhole than I was anywhere else. She lost a daughter when she was five and a half years old so maybe I was a little bit of a replacement. I don't know.

I've got a sister, she lived at home. I went to and fro really.

Like a vagrant?

Yes, that's right!

My father was a farmer. He went in to the army at the beginning of World War One. He was in France the whole of the time. He was badly wounded towards the end of 1917.

All I wanted to do when I left school was farming.

That was my life and I ignored everybody else because that's what I wanted to do. It was the last thing my father wanted me to do. Things had been bad in the thirties. Farming was very bad between the wars, it was desperately difficult. They all tried to talk me out of it but I was determined.

My very nice aunt who lived at Buckhole farm supported me through out her life – financially and in every other aspect so I was lucky in that respect. I was able to do what I wanted to do.

The first thing I did, the day I left school, was get on an old Fordson Tractor with a very ancient cultivator and I was thinking about it this morning – the implements we used were terribly old fashioned. We still had horses but we had this old Fordson tractor – not a Fergie – the Ferguson didn't come in 'til about 1948. We did have one of the first ones in about '48 – but I left school in 1945 I suppose and we had an old Fordson.

I sat on the old Fordson from 1945 until I got married really – not all the time! But it seemed to be most of the time.

Cousin Arthur, Chris Rigby and Doug

All the families around met in the pub – you could split the farming fraternity in two in those days – not so much now. The small farmers who farmed anything from 150-200 acres- they used to meet in the pubs. The pub was very much a part of farming life in those days. Harry Mortley, he kept the Fenn Bell, he was an interesting character, he's dead now though. I still meet my cousin there, Arthur Baker.

Edward Baker, my grandfather, went to Clinch Street when he was married. It was the only farm the Pye family owned, now my cousin owns it. They rented the rest of the farm in that area. Edward looked after Clinch Street Farm and the surrounding fields – he also looked after Northward Hill – which comes into the part of RSPB – the Norrad I know it as – and in spite of what the RSPB would have you believe it was a better nature reserve in those days than it is now. The rides were all cut and kept clean. He used to rear his own pheasants. My cousin will tell you how many herons there were before the war. There were more than there are now and it's supposed to be the largest Heronry in the country.

There were an enormous amount of shelduck in those days – all birds. There was all wildlife but my grandfather was anti-badger in those days – he was convinced that they spread TB and of course it is possible so he wouldn't have had a badger on the place. We had badgers at Gatton's – only one I know of at Brick House but we had a few at Gatton's.

Health care was limited –but it was good, the doctors looked after the community very well. I think we expect more now – we expect far too much. Everyone thinks they've got a right to everything and they don't, we haven't got a right to anything.

My biggest change was when I retired. I had a choice after my marriage broke down, I had to either re-finance the farm or retire. That was 7 or 8 years ago and I was 60 and I didn't feel at that age I wanted to take on further commitments. I'm sorry I did it in some ways because I miss farming very much. It was a terrible wrench.

I was used to walking out on my own fields and all of a sudden someone else is farming it. That was the biggest change in my life.

I met Sue in 1984 – just before my marriage finally broke up but Sue was nothing to do with the break up. Well you know we're living in Rochester now and I'm quite happy.

The First Interview

Doug parked the car on a track – huge barns, new and (very) old to one side, ancient pond and weeping willows to the other. Peacock feathers littered the path and ducklings scattered as we approached the 18th Century Farmhouse at Cooling Court.

In the kitchen an old range cooker is warm with a permanent soft whistle coming from the kettle on its top. A 60's Formica table stands in the middle with coffee mugs at the ready and a promising box of old photographs. Formica units under a window that overlook the pond provide a bed for a ginger cat and contrast with the ancient white painted dresser that covers the opposite wall of the kitchen and is heavily laden with matching jugs and dust. It has probably stood there since the house was built – a good 250 years.

This was Maurice Whitebread's kitchen at Cooling Court.

Maurice Whitebread

Tractors, the war and more tractors

Maurice at Cooling Court

I was born August 10th 1918 at The Mount, Rochester. My father was Arthur Edward Whitebread, my mother was Nelly. As far as I know I was brought up at The Mount. The house was adjoining the land there and my grandfather bought it. My grandfather died aged 52 in 1896 and I've still got his chequebook stubs in the bureau from the London and Provincial bank as it was then, now it's the National Westminster. That was my father's father, Thomas William and his father was Thomas William the elder.

I have the family tree going back to about 1700.

Higham and Wainscot was their farming area, but Father liked the idea of this area (Cooling Court) because it was good potato growing land and potatoes were the main crop at that time. He didn't grow much corn, only if he had a field he didn't quite know what to do with.

My father bought Cooling Court, or part of it, in 1935. There was 80 acres, my father bought 50 and, I don't know if he couldn't afford it, but there was another 30 acres right up over the hill that was known as Mill Stubbs Field.

He bought it from Frank Batchelor, who went bankrupt in 1935 – he was the son of JW Batchelor, Cocoa Billy. There were three brothers, I think they were all Methodists one was JW Batchelor, then there was Charlie Batchelor up at New Barn, and he was known as Lemonade Charlie. Then there was George Batchelor at Gatton's who was known as Hop Ale George. They got their nicknames because they were all Methodists and they wouldn't touch alcohol.

Franklin's daughter, Kathleen, said there was a huge violent rainstorm, which destroyed all their strawberries. I have a picture of the old barn showing the field of strawberries. But a lot of people said it was down to him, too much money spent on showing pigs. He had a lot of pigs with Mr. Oliver in charge.

My father paid £2000 for Cooling Court and he had to borrow that. Of course 1935 was a bad year, they had severe frosts in May in that year. He had to lay men off, all the potatoes were cut off. There was no food, all the potatoes went black, they were all cut off, that was May 18th, there was nothing like it.

What amazed me and my brother too, was that not only did he have to borrow money to buy Cooling Court, he also bought a brand new international crawler tractor, which my brother still has from 1935. It cost £350, a lot of money in those days, a Ford Standard cost £150 on cleats and £180 on rubbers. Maybe that's why he couldn't afford that 30 acres.

Tractors were coming in quite a bit by then and he already had a little Bristol crawler and quite liked it and wanted something bigger, so part-exchanged another tractor to buy it. It was an international 1020 of 1927, which was the first tractor I ever drove.

I left school at 16 and went to work on the farm. I used to help in school holidays and had to help the lad in the garden and mow the lawn. You had to have a lad then to pull the mower, as well as the man pushing, there was no such thing as motor mowers then.

I've often wondered what I would or could have done if I didn't farm. You did as your father told you in those days and anyway, what else was there to do? I was very interested in the sea but it was hardly a great living. But you see I've enjoyed every minute of it. It's been a hard grind sometimes but there you are, you get despondent, but looking back on it, what a great opportunity I've had. This is a lovely spot (Cooling Court) every one admires it.

During the war father let it (Cooling Court) to a friend Christopher Cuckney a greengrocer with a shop in North Street, Strood. My father wanted to pull the house down, because it had become so dilapidated, and build something more practical. But an architect from Gravesend, George Clay, worked on it. I didn't know then about listed buildings.

Corn was a very low price after the war, wheat was about £25/ton for best wheat, the government made it up to £30. Barley, I bought in at £18 when I had the pigs.

Maurice , Man and Machine

When we joined the common market, corn prices rocketed and when you fed those sorts of prices to the pigs, the price you got for the pigs just didn't reflect it. People just had to give up. Everyone around here had a few pigs, I bought a few geldings from poor old Tom Crawford.

I have a brother (Donald), he was farming, and father set him up at Grove Farm in Higham during the war. It was about 30 acres and he did quite well up there. It was high ground and he didn't get frost so much on his potatoes and fruit. I often got despondent when I saw the sort of huge crops he was getting and mine had all been hit by frost.

Wheat, barley and oats all had to be shocked, it depended how big the crop was as to the size of the shock. You had to build shocks up so that the prevailing wind would blow through and dry it out. In 1958 we had to throw the whole lot down and re-shock because of the rain. In 58 it rained and rained, they got so wet from the inside and had to be dried out. It can get very hot in the middle, you had to watch it and let it dry out. If a stack got too hot you'd have to open it out to get dry and then re-stack. It should stack dry.

If it was stacked right then you'd have the threshing machine proprietor and thresh it out into 2 cwt sacks – a steam engine! Later on they had a tractor to run the thresher, the contractor was George May from Chatham. Very reasonably priced and you'd get help from your neighbours because it was quite a job and you'd need help. The contractor himself was usually the feeder, her fed the machine and there was a girl who'd pass the sheaf to him with the knife under the string, she would snatch the string as he took it and collect a big bundle of it. Mr. Harrison was farming over here, we got together with him, his mans name was Brian Sears.

Father set me up here when I came out of the army in 1946. I was called up with the militia in 1939, I was between 20 and 21, everyone had to go then, you weren't exempted, although later people in farming were exempted. Although I must say that I was given a stay of call up because I had to get the harvest in. I should have gone in the August and I think I went in September. It was before the war started and there were no reserved occupations, you jolly well had to go. I went to Edinburgh to the Calvary depot of the Scots Greys. I still have my sword and bandolier and spurs – all I'd done with horse before that was probably just sitting on one, a little cob!

We did training at Red Barracks in Edinburgh at the foot of the Pentland Hills. Then when we had completed our training, we were posted to Colchester to prepare for going abroad, Palestine. But then, we held a mounted parade and with new, different horses, mine reared up on me. I fell off over the back and the horse rolled on me and I broke a wrist – so I was in hospital in Colchester and didn't get to

Palestine then. After that the cavalry were being disbanded and we became the nucleus of the Royal Armoured Corps. So I finished my army service in the RAC's.

We got to Egypt eventually but the war was mostly over by then. I suppose I was lucky really, there were a number of people who were serving with me who never came back. I used to correspond with one gentleman a little older than me. We used to exchange Christmas cards but then I didn't get one from him and had a letter from his wife to tell me he had died.

I was demobilised and came back in 1945 and helped my father out at Noke Street Farm and then father said would you like to take over at Cooling Court – I said 'yes please'. When we got to the house, my word, my wife was frightened, we had nothing to put in it. Mother and father gave us some second hand carpets and old bits of furniture.

I met my wife in the army at Tadworth. She was working for the NAAFI, she wasn't a local girl, and she was from Yorkshire. She took to farming very well, she settled very well. If I had to do any seed sowing she would round up the pigs, because of course we had a number of breeding pigs here at that time. We had 45 breeding sows and a farrowing house at the back to do the job properly. We'd fatten some, sell some off as weaners, all sorts of things.

We stopped the pigs – common market, that wrecks everything. My wife would pay off all the casual workers and that sort of thing.

I have a son, Graham, he runs the farm now. It's his life, he couldn't wait to get on a tractor. I have a photo of him when he could hardly reach the pedals. It gets in your blood.

When we started we had three full time men and my niece used to look after the pigs. Then in the last fifteen years of my running the farm, we had nobody. I just did it myself, arable and combining and everything; of course it's only a small acreage here. Noke Street was divided up when Father died. So my brother and I had half each of that. We had a sister but she died just the year after my wife died. Father gave her some house property to balance out, to make things even. That's how it is.

My brother married a land army girl (Peta Harvey), because we had quite a few Land Girls at Noke Street, but father had a manager there. They came from all over the place. They were directed into it – they either had to join the

Waafs or ATD or they had to do something. Munitions or Land Army or VAD's. Yes, there was quite a selection and like men they were directed – some (men) went into mining. I had a friend directed into mining.

They took to it quite well, I had a girl here for some time, and she had lodgings up at the Horseshoe and Castle. Farming was an essential industry after the war and when you think of it, farming is the vital industry in the whole world.

Peta was at Noke Street Farm. Noke Street and Blacklands were together then. Blacklands Farm was where my father was born; my nephew's living in it now. Peta and Donald were married and she just got on with things. Her great love is flower arranging now. They go in for competitions and she decorates the church for special occasions. I think she's a steward at the ploughing match, she has a flower-arranging stall there.

I was involved with the ploughing match for almost as long as I've been farming. I used to do the vintage tractor class for 25 years but I can't tramp over the fields like I used to so I've handed on to my son with Mr Hunt from Gore Street Farm. They'll keep it going for a while – it's the biggest class in the ploughing match now. You see the big tractors on the farms now, one tractor replaces three of the old ones and there's not the men who want to go to the competition nowadays. I think they call it Classic Class now. What I call a modern tractor, 30 years old, they're bringing in a special class. The Ploughing match has been going about 200 years. It's a good idea for the ploughmen to pit their skills against each other. The farmers were keen on it.

Ploughing Match Moat farm – 1948

I remember the plough was loaded up on to the horse-drawn corn wagon and there might be two horses pulling it.

The Wagoner's family were in the wagon and the spare horse walked behind on a halter. It was important to have a good day out. They started ploughing at 8 in the morning, nowadays its 10 am. Wagoners used to be up all night before a match getting everything and the horses ready. There'd be corn and vegetables and we used to have a fruit stand then. There were trade stands but there are more people coming in now to do demos and things, it's more commercialised.

■■■

A big ginger cat lands amongst the photographs and Maurice asks if we'd like to see his tractors. We go out to the shed, renovated machines gleam from under covers. Maurice has a small museum of vintage machines lovingly restored, some of which still compete in the local ploughing match. I later learn that Donald, his brother , has a similar passion that he invests in motorbikes.

Charlie and Doris Keats

Farming, the Homeguard, Courting and work at the big house.

A seventies bungalow is home to Charlie and Doris Keats. Charlie worked on Doug's Farm at Gatton's. Doris and Charlie sit close on the sofa, Doris lays her small hand on Charlies thigh and he covers it with his.

Charlie. I'm Charlie Edward Keats, I was born in Allhallows on 10th February 1922. My father came from Allhallows but I don't know much else about my parents. He worked with stock, other people's sheep and all that on Allhallows marshes during the 1914-1918 war. I was born there and left there before I was five years old, so I don't remember too much about his past. His father was a policeman. I never knew my grandfather but I did know my granny.

She used to live at Grain and that was our yearly holiday. We used to go and stay there and if we used to play up she would come up the stairs at us with two sticks. She would never miss, there was no fear of that. We didn't used to go very often because we used to have to either walk thereor Dad used to get a chap by the name of Reynolds who had a motorbike and sidecar and he used to run us down there.

The first place I can remember we went to was near Wainscot, a place called Whitebread's. He worked for the Whitebread's in 1927. And he worked for Gatton's. He was still in stock, a shepherd and he looked after cattle.

I started school at the little Cooling Street School when I was five, that's next door to us now. I suppose there was thirty in one class, and forty in another class, sometimes. There were three classrooms. Children came from Tooley Street farm and others who lived locally.

When I was eleven I went to the church school at Cliffe. We used to have to walk from here up there to school when I was fourteen. In those days if your father worked on the farm then you went to work on the farm, as did my brothers and stepbrothers. My stepbrothers before me worked there and then they left and went into the army. I stayed with my father. It was expected. All the farms around here belonged to the Batchelors – Batchelors this and Batchelors that, so you automatically had to go where your father worked. It was like an apprenticeship – I grew up with it. I went to work at Gattons when I left school.

My first day at work I just went with my father and learnt how to open and shut gates. I had always been with him since I was a boy and I knew what his job was and my Father used to be a heavy drinker. As long as he had a shilling he was in the pub, so half his time, as long as he was in the pub, I used to do half his work. So, at weekends, he had a few drinks on a Friday night and went to work on the Saturday and then go to the pub on Saturday night. By Sunday morning he couldn't face it so I used to do it, when I was twelve or thirteen. He knew about it – I used to milk the cows and so on, I never knew anything else.

I quite enjoyed school. I wasn't well educated, you weren't in those days, but it wasn't too bad. We used to walk across the fields but when you did that you'd end up with horse collars over your shoulder to take to the saddlers up at Cliffe to get them mended for the farmer.

My mother worked out on the land. We never knew any other life. You didn't have a holiday, you had to make your own. You didn't have a lot to do with children outside the family. Some old farm labourers used to be a bit grudging to one another working on different farms. If you worked on a farm it was like belonging to a football team. My father said we shouldn't go with other kids.

I started work for the Batchelor's in 1936 and used to do all these jobs. I think he used to give out £32 a week. I used to get 10 shillings and a halfpenny a week. I would get a ten-shilling note and a penny one week and just the ten-shilling note the next.

Mother used to take most of the money. She'd give us back 2 bob, the old florin.

The Batchelor's farmed, more or less, with the family. They'd been there all the time. I knew the old lady. The Father had died and the sons, I think there were four or five of them, all ran the farm and the oldest one, Arthur George, hired all the workmen.

Arthur George was really good, he was like a sergeant major, but you went to work for him and you worked for him! They looked after us. When we were kids, at Christmas, the old lady, Arthur's Mother, who we used to take the milk to up at the house every morning, she would give you a tin of toffees or a book or something like that. She was quite a Victorian, with the long black skirt and high neck. Quite a decent old lady though.

I worked for Arthur and he had Sharnel Street, and I had to bike there, even in the snow, across the meadows, it used to be all grass on the bank above the station and we used to do the lambing up there. We had anything up to 300, 400 or even 500 lambing ewes up there. In January and February time you used to be lambing. If it snowed you couldn't get round the roads, so we used to walk up the railway line to get there.

They'd lamb in the fields, they used to build little straw huts and if it was too bad we used to stop there. We had an ordinary shed there with oil lamps. I remember my father used to go up to the Red Dog and leave me in the shed. He would have two or three beers and come back and sit on his box and nod off. His head would droop and his chin would go on his chest and then he would fly back and I used to wait for that, to watch him fly back.

Every lamb you got you used to get sixpence so we took a lot of care. We had hessian sacking and even if it was really rough we used to wrap the lambs up in sacking as soon as they were born and dry them off. We used to thatch the gates around the top round the compound to protect them from the weather. I've seen triplets born, and if one ewe lost a lamb you would take one of the triplets, re-coat it with the lamb's skin and give it to the other ewe.

During the summer there was only enough work for my father so I used to work with the horses. As I became eighteen the war broke out and I volunteered for the army and the day I was due to go my exemption papers arrived saying my father had exempted me, as I was needed on the land.

I was wild about it and said to my father I was going on with it, all my mates were going to war, but I was exempted so that was it.

It was hard work during the winter. I used to have a bike. I started in the morning at ten past six.. I used to bike to Clinch Street and on to Sharnel Street and I used to have to feed all the bullocks because he used to have the sheep to do. I did that then I used to have to find my way back and mix up all the feed for the next time. I thought I wouldn't bother anymore. The boss came up to me and said,

'You're leaving are you?'

I said, 'Yes, I've had enough of this'

So he said; 'If you're going you better take your mother and father with you'

They'd been there for twenty years, so that's how it came about I stayed, I had no choice. Then he said,

'I'll tell you what, I've got a brand new tractor in the shed, I'll teach you how to go on that'

I still helped my father but I did tractor work too. I used to run to and from Sharnel Street on the tractor. I stayed doing that and then, when I worked for Doug, we got the modern tractor.

Charlie pauses and gathers his thoughts.

Arthur Batchelor died and his son Peter took on the farm, but he was the opposite of his father. Whereas Arthur had been the sergeant major, a money making man, Peter was like a fairy godmother, he was just the opposite. He would say,

'You do what I tell you. How you do it is up to you, you know how to do it and you do it'.

So that's how it was. He was a very gentle man, like a fairy godmother, such a nice fellow. He would go away for a week but he'd give you work to do. If he came along and you were sitting down, perhaps having a cup of tea, he would say,

'Don't you get up because I've come along'

That was his attitude.

He used to have real old do's down at the old house, the yachting crew and all that down there. You would get up in the morning and find the fence across the drive!

He really enjoyed life. When he came here with his wife back from Cambridge they hit an army lorry and he nearly lost his wife and kiddie, Christopher. They were badly injured but survived, but Peter's marriage didn't. He was about my age Peter.

Our children played together. After Arthur died, and Peter took over, his mother and sister were there so when he moved into Gatton's, they moved out. His sister was there all the time though. She used to work in London during the war – she was 10 years older, Holly.

She worked for the Agriculture ministry, I think, something like that. They used to take her to the train every morning. I've stayed in touch with her.

After Peter separated from his first wife and married his second he went away on honeymoon and had a heart attack. We never saw him again for three months.

Peter had two sons from his first wife, Christopher and Graham, but he didn't want them to take over. He didn't get on with Christopher. It didn't matter which Batchelor you spoke to they were always afraid someone was going to overthrow them. The Batchelors were always feuding. Roy took over one farm and Guy took over after Roy. Christopher thought he would get Sharnel Street and then Doug took it over.

There were only four of us left then, after Peter's heart attack there was a manager and he ran things right down, got rid of quite a few men.

I was worried when new management took over, it was such a contrast. I'd been on the same patch for all these years and done as I liked all the time.

Doug says, 'Charlie taught me to farm Gatton's'

We had plenty of machinery but not on Doug's scale. We were hiring combines – Doug had brand new tractors, whereas we were used to old pen tractors with no head cover or anything like that. But we just did it like you were used to and Doug was satisfied with that.

Doug says, ' Charlie taught me about knowing the soil as well as the land'

Well, I did it all the time. All my work with Batchelor's, I did all the potatoes and crops and I did the ploughing too. I did ploughing matches with the horses.

After I got married we had eight children and we managed on our farm pay. We didn't owe any money and we had nothing on HP unlike some people who were on better wages. My wife came from Wainscott.

Doris. My father was Tommy Horne, a gamekeeper, and he came to work for Brice's at Mockbeggar in Cliffe Woods. I used to work for Mrs. Brice and do all the odd jobs and waited on table, and she wanted me to carry on working for her when I got married but I was living in there and when I got married we went to Cooling to live.

We got married in 1942. Before that I knew Joe Brice very well and I used to work for Mrs Joan, for three days a week, up at the Knowle sometimes when I wasn't working for Mrs. Brice. Simon Brice was born at the Knowle but they weren't there for very long.

When I worked in the house and they used to have shoots, Mr. Brice had a friend to stay who had two golden eagles and many a time he sat at the dining table with one on his right shoulder, we weren't to worry as we always served from the left, as you should, and it wouldn't move when you walked behind him. May was the cook then.

During the war we slept in the cellars in case of raids. Even Mr and Mrs Brice slept in the cellar. Charlie was in the home guard then.

Charlie: I used to go on duty at 9 o'clock and one night I called in first- at Mockbeggar House - and it was raining. Maurice Gill, who married one of the Brice daughters came in - they lived in Frindsbury - and of course you weren't supposed to wear your uniform unless you were on duty so he asked what I was doing there. I said I had called into see my young lady and he packed me off and I got a reprimand for it.

We used to work all day, got home 8 or 9 o'clock at night, put your uniform on and go and sit on a sea wall all night, get up next morning and off you'd go again. If you weren't working at the weekend you'd be in the army. My wife lived at Cliffe Lodge, where Cliffe Grange is by Mockbeggar, and when her father became gamekeeper and her brothers left home he moved to Silver Street so that he was close to the woods. They had big shoots. Cobb had it before the Brice's.

Doris: Where Mockbeggar farm offices are now was always the office and there was a cottage on the other side where the chauffeur who drove Mrs. Brice about lived years ago and the little white bungalow that has been converted at the top of Lee Green is where the gardener lived. Mr and Mrs. Seager lived there.

Charlie: I remember one night when the stables caught fire. We went in and got two of the horses out but they had a pony there and we couldn't get that one.

Charlie and Doris look down at their clasped hands.

Frank Reginald Hammond

Running water, blacksmiths and theivin'

Mr and Mrs Frank Hammond

I was born on 1st September 1927 at Middle Stoke.
Dad was a Stoke man, born in Stoke and lived there all his
life. When he joined the army he was posted at Woolwich
barracks and that was where he met my Mother. She at that
time was working at Siemens the cable people in Woolwich.
She lived in Charlton and I think the factory was in
Woolwich, where the barracks were. Of course, like a lot of
people do, they met and got married eventually.

She was born in 1889, so they probably married around 1909. They came down here in 1913, to Middle Stoke, because by then they had my eldest sister, Rosie and they lived at the Anchorage in Middle Street , which is no longer there, there's a housing estate there now. Then they got this place at Middle Stoke which was called Jimmy Muggeridge's Cottages and we eventually ended up with 10 of us there - 8 children and Mum and Dad in four rooms – amazing isn't it?

I'm the youngest of them, of four boys and four girls – when they had me that was it, things just got worse and worse!

Mum worked on the fields and did God knows what to make ends meet. The old man, when the first oil tanks were built at Grain, the power petrol place, the storage tanks belonged to the Admiralty – they were built in 1912 – the power plant was built in 1923. Anyway, the old man went there, he was a steel erector, putting the tanks up. That's all he did mainly and when that was built he worked on the council for a while and eventually he finished up with the R & A D down at Port Victoria, which was just prior to the war. They knew that the war was coming and then he was working down there when he died in 1949.

My Mum went on working on the farm; she worked for Doug's Dad up at Brick House. She worked at part of Dagnam's before then, before the war. I think she worked on most of the farms. They used to walk to all of the farms. The old man, when he was on the dole, which they very often were in those days, he used to have to walk to Binney's to dig potatoes by hand.

Unknown, Orchard near Rochester.

Dad would go out at 6 o'clock and mum would get us all ready for school and she would walk to Binney or wherever at 8 o'clock and dig potatoes or whatever and then she would come home at night and do our dinner. We would all be home. It's not like these days when you can go home and there'd be no one there.

Doug's Uncle Bill lived in Kitchenor Cottage. These house were built just after the war in 1924 or so and named after General Kitchenor. Then he took over the Nag in 1929. I remember because I was two when I moved to Kitchenor cottages. A chap called Harry Barnes was there before that. I didn't go there until I was five and that's when we had electric light put in the village of Stoke.

I remember the first night my mother lifted me up to turn on the light at Kitchenor Cottages. You associated things with what you did and that was when we moved there. So of course when we got to Kitchenor Cottages and we had water indoors we could look to Middle Stoke where all the water had to be carried indoors from a tank and the toilet was a bucket one which was right up the garden – very handy in the middle of January.

Kitchenor Cottages had a bath indoors and taps with water coming out which was fascinating for me – we kept filling the bath up because we couldn't believe it. We had to take turns getting the clean water before – if you were lucky you got in first and had the clean water – the last one got the dregs. It's a world that you can't really believe. In a few years it had all changed.

Before that there was no water laid on indoors, no electric, no gas - just an old coal fire in the kitchen that was your living room as well.

Our toilet was normally an orange box with a little bit of curtain pulled across it and mum told me, at night time, we'd pull the stairs up to stop the rats coming in – there was a ditch opposite us then full of rats. People say there's a lot of rats nowadays but I never see them.

So we moved to Kitchenors Cottages and that's where I stayed until I eventually married in 1966.

Before that I started working in 1941 at the old power plant when I was fourteen and worked in the laboratory for a spell with a chap called Ernie Ridley. I didn't go much on that, the fumes didn't do my chest any good and I finished up with a bloke named Figgy and a bloke named Eric Cross from High Halstow who was a carpenter until 1949 when Anglo-Iranian came in and that's when I started with them and in 1952 I started shift work in the refinery.

I was called an operator. We all started at the bottom, unlike today where you start at the top. We went to school for about twelve weeks and were taught what a refinery did, not just about oil but about the power – I didn't know half what they were teaching me – I was operating machinery which could handle say one million gallons of crude oil a week, 8,000 gallons a day or something like that.

They taught me how to handle valves and pumps and what the chemical reaction was. They taught me all this at the school. A chap named Grimstock taught me. Some were brighter than others and they got the top jobs but gradually, as we got older, we less intelligent, we took longer to get there but, eventually, we made it. In that sort of job you progress or you don't progress.

They didn't make you take the Foreman's job, they asked if you would like it and you said yes or no. I said yes but if it was any benefit or not I don't know.

That went on from 1952 to 1982 when they shut it down. They were very kind about remuneration when they closed it but from 1982 I didn't go to work anymore. I was 55 when I retired – it seems a nice age to say goodbye to work.

My mum had a job at the refinery. She worked there in the canteen which she enjoyed – the easiest job she ever had and she worked there until she was 76 – they had to force her to go out the door and that was the finish of her, she was so popular down there, being an old lady, and they thought a lot of her.

In the village she was Aunt Rose, in those days every village had an 'Aunt'. When mum was younger and we were children we had Granny Craddock as we called her. She used to be the midwife, called for illness, lancing boils, carbuncles, the lot – Old Granny Craddock. and mum later in life – well when one old girl goes another takes over, and mum was Aunt Rose to most people. They will say now,

'Oh Aunt Rose, yes, I remember her alright'.

When I got married to Jodie she thought mum was not like a mother-in-law really, she was more like a granny to her because of the age difference. Mum lived quite a few years after packing up at the oil refinery, she didn't die until she was 87 – so this saying that hard work kills you - well! She had 8 children and worked the fields and God knows what and whether she would have lived longer if she hadn't done that – well, I don't know!

It's a job to think of all that's happened since 1927 'til now. It only seems like 5 minutes.

In those days in Middle Stoke an old boy lived next door to us, Nick Lesley, and he used to say to Mum, knowing she had 8 children and we couldn't afford a lot, 'Don't get any meat this week Mrs. Hammond, I've got a sheep. He's been out on the marsh and I've caught him'. The sheep had died so we had lamb for a week – he would skin it and cut it up.

Over the road was Cyril Cherry who would catch fish down by the Medway. You could eat fish, and he would say to my dad in the pub – 'Do you want a fish Toby? (his nickname) and in the morning that fish would be hanging on a nail on the back door. Even when we moved to Kitchenor Cottages that still happened. Flat Fish they were, flounders. They used to call him Flounder, perhaps that's why.

You didn't have to go to town for much then. In the village there were two butchers and you could always get two pennyworth of meat. You would go to Mrs Bett and mum would get meat.

Dad was gassed in the war and got a little pension. Not much, only a pound a week or so, but a pound a week was what I got in 1941 for a weeks work. We always had meat and we had puddings – I haven't had one since I got married. I remember those meat puddings.

For milk we used to go to Bennett's farm, old Dick Bennett. He had cows up and down the lane and we used to be sent up to get the milk from Mrs Bennett, Sally Bennett. Four pints of skimmed milk – not to be healthy, it was cheaper than full cream.

A lady lived next door to us, George Harbour the wheelwright and Amy Harbour, she was a Muggeridge before she was married, she was very good to mum. She would always help mum out In my case clothes were easy because my aunt, my mums sister, used to be in service with a family named Parry from South Africa and their lad was about the same age as me and the same build and he used to go to private school and used to change his clothes every six months so I used to have a parcel come quite regularly.

I was always the best dressed kid in the village! I was O.K. until he started wearing plus fours -that was a bit over the top. It was quite funny, but it's only thinking back I remember these things. Anyway the fish and the meat were always on call, and there was always someone who, well, in those days thieving was a way of life.

It was a way of making sure you had enough food. It wasn't fair on the farmers and people who had these things but to me it was a way of life where I was brought up. Nick Lesley was a robber. They were real characters when you think about it.

There were all sorts with big families then – the Gardeners, the Woods opposite, Mr. Woods was the blacksmith in Middle Stoke. The blacksmiths shop belonged to Johnny Woods' dad until the war when he packed it up. In those days there was a lot of forge work going on in the fields, horses' feet for a start. It's not on the same scale today. When Woods packed up, Uncle Albert, who had the village blacksmith in Stoke, he did the lot then. All the Betts' horses - 14 of them - and the Muggeridges'- another dozen – a lot of horses to be shod in those days. Then there was George Harbour the wheelwright, he used to rule the forge in Middle Stoke – he used to make all the Muggeridge carts.

Doug; I remember he used to wheel them through the village. Kent carts they were.

Of course when Betts moved here he had Lincolnshire carts. They were a different shape. I don't think George Harbour made them.

Apart from that he made all the coffins for people who had died – he was the undertaker as well. No one liked to see George Harbour walking down the street with a ruler in his hand.

The village was very self-supportive. Goldsmith had the Empire Butchers as we called it. He would kill all his own meat. Every Monday they would all come in and it would break my heart to hear all those pigs until they were slaughtered, but we ate them, I know. Goldsmith didn't have any local meat, he had Empire, so he was called the Empire Butcher.

Then we had Lingfield bread or Stone's bread. The
actual grocers shop was Parker and that was in High Halstow
– he had a branch in Stoke. Then we had Reynolds – he was
a real grocer trained by Vye's in Rochester. Then we had a
shoe repairer, Bradley's, a barbers opposite Harold Bradley
who used to charge up accumulators and things for your
radio – and we had Thomas from the east End of London
who we used to call the old Jew Boy, but he used to have his
shop out front, I remember all the barrels and lino – wine- he
had the lot. Thomas Mallen who used to work in the actual
workshop , cart repairing, he had nuts, bolts, nails. Mrs
Thomas had the drapers – anything you wanted in that line.

People came round from town as well, a lot of our shopping was brought in by carriers – like Doug's Uncle Bill and George Mortley. He did the coal as well. All our stuff would come into Stoke Siding in the train days. Mum would use it – it were no bother coming down from London in those days because the train was always there. It started coming to Sharnel Street in 1882 and Stoke in 1889 and then it was extended for Queen Victoria *(authors note: right to the coast to facilitate a Royal Visit).*

It was easier to come from Woolwich in those days than getting to Chatham nowadays.

There were no antibiotics then so you had to take your luck. When you wanted to see the doctor you had to book an appointment to see Dr. Wall and his surgery was over at Mrs. Thomas's. If you were a drinker, or even if you were just 14, they'd say,

'You go down to Mrs. Marsh and have a glass of stout with mead and tell her I'll pay her when I get down there'.

Whether he did or not I don't know because old Polly would give her heart away.

It's amazing the changes we have seen over the years but we survived.

The doctor would come once a week, if it was urgent you used to have to go to Hoo on the bus or if you were lucky, someone would take you by car. Not many people had a car in those days – you could play in the street all day, only horses and carts about.

Old Albert Hammond lost a lot of his family to TB. He was a good blacksmith, he had 8 children – not like us, my Dad went away and got married to someone else so the actual blood strain was different but a lot of people married locally and they all ended up tied together because they were all related on both sides.

Uncle Albert married a Collins girl, they were all incorporated, but Uncle Albert was all right. Clarice, Rita and Hector were the three who died of TB. Archie was saved by the new drug, Streptomycin. He was one of the guinea pigs to have that and he was lucky because it saved him. Archie was the only one who didn't marry local of that lot. Bert married a Sullivan, Betty, Peter's older sister and Hector married a Bloomfield. There was nothing wrong in it but that's why the TB was all in Uncle Albert's family and the Collin's. It was a well known thing in that particular family – this strain of TB.

I don't know how I survived as a kid – I had pneumonia and pleurisy twice. Mum said it was Dr Cecil, Dr. Wall's son that saved me. The second time I got bad was when I was 4 – I got teased about it but I hated missing school. I'd be done in but I still didn't want to miss school.

The teachers Williams and Jenkins lived opposite me in the little cottage Mrs Oates had, where the tennis courts were. Joycie and Wilf Plewis and all those used to play tennis. Williams and Jenkins were two ladies from Wales – they sound it don't they? I think they were before their time those two – they enjoyed each others company, but the less said the better.

Amy Harbour taught me in Infants, and she taught my Dad in the infants' class, that's how long she was at the school.

People moaned about her being Church, she always ran everything – well someone had to didn't they? She and Vera Muggeridge were both long livers. The Muggeridge's farmed from Fenn Wood right through to the Isle of Grain; Dickie Muggeridge at Grain, Arthur Muggeridge at Turkey Hall, Freddie Muggeridge at Hoo – they farmed nearly all of it though the church owned it. Oh and Jimmy Muggeridge at Mackey's Court.

During the war we only did half a day at school, us in the morning, Allhallows in the afternoon. That's how I ended up as thick as I am, half as bright as I should have been. Had I been educated I would have been dangerous.

The other half a day Betts at Upper Stoke would use the lads to clean out the stables. You'd get half a crown for that and it was a lovely half crown to have. You could buy all the fags you wanted for the week, pit yourself in the Nags and play bar billiards. When you left school at 14 there's not much time for anything else but work. All my mates left at 14 – it was normal routine of life and you just got on with it.

All the Hammonds were blacksmiths. Uncle Bill, Mary's Dad at Middle Street, Uncle Albert (Hammond) was. He worked hard. I remember he won a few hundred quid on the football pools, I don't remember how much exactly, but after that he had this desire to be rich and it drove him mental. I remember him being mental.

I used to feel sorry for the horses, he was a cruel man to some of the animals. I could weep. The shires and the carthorse had feet like dinner plates, bigger even, like dustbin lids. They used to fill up the blacksmiths shop at the back and when they cut their feet off they used to throw the bits to the dogs. A lot of dogs they had. I was allowed to go in and pump the fire because he was my Uncle. I used to pump the flue and the old boy, little old Stumpy Watson, used to sit and watch me.

All the old boys used to sit there. If you couldn't get into the Ship or if you couldn't afford a drink, the blacksmiths was out of the wind on that corner. A proper old place, 400 or 500 years old.

My dad was a blacksmith but he never took it up. Dad was in the RASC in the war but he just dealt with horses, he didn't blacksmith them. He didn't want it, he went into the engineering side. I did engineering too.

Sometimes we follow the father's footsteps like the old song. I don't think I really followed mine. I used to drink but never at the old mans level. He'd go to work at 6 and come home at 8, drunk.

In those days, well, talk about out of hours drinking, the Nag's Head had boarders. There was Big Harry who's buried in the chapel. I remember as a kid going to his funeral, they played the Last Post over him. There was

Freddy Miles – he used to get drunk for six weeks at a time; he'd stay down the Nags and drink and drink and drink and then, after six or seven weeks, he would all of a sudden stop and go home and his wife would square him up. He never had enough money on him. They lived in that little building that's outside the Nag now, where the bus stop is. There was a fireplace in the kitchen, not much room, with a bed in each corner.

Then there was old Aaron Edwards who slept at the pub. He used to do odd jobs – hoeing and so on. He used to be allowed to sleep in the pub because he was cleaner than the rest of them. There was a peep through door in the passageway of the Nag's Head where you ordered beer to take away. If you stood there at night like the youngsters used to, Aaron would come by with his tin bucket, in case it was required during the night shift, and with an alarm clock with him. Every night he did that all through the 1940's. We used to shout 'Here comes Aaron' and all stand out the way and let him go up the little steps and disappear thorough the door every night.

I remember Con Saville, my uncle. The Savilles and Hammonds were half brothers. I've got one in Grain still,

Ernie Saville – he's still there. Ned used to be in the Ship didn't he? Used to drive all the swill from the dockyard all round the pig farms. If you went to see Uncle Con he'd meet you at the door with his shotgun. He lived in Windmill Cottages. He had a small holding up near Mackey's Meadow, a little place where the allotments were, up the top he had two or three of them by the stile. His little field was on the right, with his shed and he always had a pony.

Years ago Uncle Con and my old man used to go up on a Sunday round Cliffe and he used to go on this one particular pony and trap because he knew the way home. He had to know the way home because they could never have driven home! They used to go all round Cliffe and Cooling in the pony and cart and the pony would bring them home. A proper little cart with a back door. It would cost a fortune now. I think there was an Irish strain in Con.

I think the ancestors must have had a touch of the Irish.

John Miskin Prior

On the notorious Pye family.

My mother was a Miskin – she was the elder daughter of William Love Miskin and Ellen Anne – they lived at Newlands from 1873 until 1894 when he died. They had 8 sons and 2 daughters. They farmed Newlands, opposite the Fenn Bell Public House.

Doug: Edith was a notorious Miskin. If you brushed with her in the magistrates court you were in serious trouble. She once ran someone over in her car and then had them up in the magistrate's court.

Yes – I saw her once, during the war, in Strood High Street, which was always choc-a-bloc. I was walking down there visiting other relations in Strood and there was an army convoy held up in both directions. It was caused by Aunt Edith doing a three, or possibly ten point turn in the middle of Strood High Street. She was larger than life altogether. She had one daughter, Helen, who married but had no children and she was a formidable woman as well. She lived at Gads Hill and finished her life as executor of Emeline Pye's will.

Emeline had £6000 in her bank account, which was a lot of money in those days, and she would pick a couple of figs from the tree and go and sell them in the market to get a few pennies. She was notoriously mean. The residue of her will went to the benefit of professional people in need of a holiday, that sort of thing. Not a cat's home as everyone thought. Helen administered it.

Helen went to Shorne, to Pond Peace, she built a house she called Broadwood, where two or three people would go and stay for longer or shorter periods who were in some kind of need. When I was chaplain at Huggins College one of the people living there from Northfleet went to Broadwood to stay when they were exhausted from working in the parish. It was like a holiday home in Shorne, built from the proceeds of Emmeline's will. Helen ran it for 10 or possibly 15 years. She lived in an adjoining house and ran it and did all the cooking – she was a very good cook.

She was Emmeline's niece and she was trusted to carry out her wishes, which she did. It was wound up eventually and Broadwood was sold. Helen died in 1974 but she may have administered the income until she died – I think it went to another charity.

Doug. My grandfather was a farm bailiff for Henry Pye and my cousin used to have to take her figs because he was landlord and staked a claim on the figs. We have here conflicting stories about Miss Pye – if it's the same one who lived at Broadwood?

Yes, Henry Pye had 4 surviving children, Emmeline, Marion, Edith and Harry (Henry Pye Junior) – who was not very capable I think, but whether he was just squashed by an overbearing father I don't know.

I didn't know Marion Pye. I saw her once – she broke her hip and could never really bend after that. Aunt Edith would take her round in the car with her hat sticking out of the sun roof because she couldn't sit in the car properly. Marion was very nice as far as I know – she lived in St. Helens in Sharnel Street. Edith became Mrs Fitchcock.

I was five when my great Uncle Walter died. He was an elderly man, very relaxed, affable and very generous.

He did fit into the Squire Miskin role – he may well have been strict with his workers but he was actually the soul of generosity and his wife was the most extravagant person you've ever met. She was Kate Hyles. Two brothers married two sisters so she was my mother's aunt on my mother's side and he was her uncle on her father's side. She and my Aunt Pauline were educated by Uncle Walter and Aunt Kate. They were members of the Royal Society of St. Anne which ran a huge orphanage at Redhill and they went to that.

Aunt Kate was generous in every way. She was a wonderful hostess and a splendid cook – she bubbled with life and jollity. She laughed all the time – she was enormously fat. Anybody who ever met Aunt Kate always laughed when she was mentioned. A new Beluncle was built after the fire there and I have quite a lot of the furniture from Beluncle. My mother kept a catalogue of things saved from the fire and they only just got out onto the roof. They rescued the sideboard, the plate basket, the thermometer and various other things. They pulled everything out of the French windows and then they got trapped upstairs.

Aunt Kate had an invalid son, Sydney. I don't know quite what was wrong with him – it was worse than that Downs Syndrome, something like autism perhaps because he was violent at times. He died in 1908. The dreadful thing was that he had to be looked after at home. They had a nurse who did that in those days and it was a dreadful thing, she had separated from her husband and was in disgrace for it for the rest of her life in a way. Ida Young was her name, Sydney called her Dodier.

Uncle Walter had pupils, one of whom, Jack King, would have liked to marry my mother, though Aunt Kate had different ideas. The Royal Engineers beagles met there and she would have produced the most wonderful food. It is reputed that his farmers in about 1928/29 clubbed together to pull him out of bankruptcy, because they liked him so much.

Robert Betts of Court Lodge at Stoke, Uncle Walter and Aunt Kate were a sort of triangle. She was very fond of Uncle Bert as I called him. He wasn't married – he was Phillip Betts' uncle.

One day the three of them were at the races and a man came along and held the gate open for them all to come through. Uncle Bert said as they passed through, 'A fine looking couple aren't they' to which the stranger replied, 'I don't know sir, I haven't finished looking at her yet'. She used to play tennis and, apart from the fact she couldn't move around the court very much, she was actually quite good.

Richard Filmer

*On farming, travel, the Homeguard and being a truly
terrible shot.*

I live at Allens Farm, Cliffe - we have done for three
or four generations now. My grandfather was a bailiff in
Sleeing at the turn of the century and he came up here just
after to start farming at Court Sole farm. He had some 30
acres there which he owned. Most of it was marshland, only
5 or 6 acres of arable. He expanded the farm to about 80 or
90 acres. He still rented at the time and started doing dairy
work and odds and sods.

My father took it on when my grandfather died in 1933
and my father expanded the farm to 90 odd acres. In 1941 or
42 he took over Manor Farm which is adjacent to where I
live now — Jim Robertson was the farmer there. He took it
over from him on his death which quadrupled the size of the
farm.

He then went off and rented another farm from the
Blue Circle Cement Co., as it is now, it was APCM then, at
Snodland, which got swallowed up in a chalk pit. In 1950 we
took on a farm in Bluebell Hill which we still have – that

was also rented from Blue Circle. I ran that in partnership with my father together with this farm here, then when my brothers got older, they were seven or eight years younger than me, they took over this farm at Bluebell Hill while I gradually increased my freehold with Douglas Marsh at Gatton's farm.

Over a period of 30 years or so we went to about 1200 acres. My father could happily cope with that. They worked very hard. Land came up and it was cheap to rent. My father took over Manor Farm in 1941 or 42 at £2 per acre to rent.

The farmers he took over from had died. The rent stayed at £2 right up until 1968 or 69 when we split the partnership up. He did it as a fixed thing because the land was released for mineral rights to Blue Circle so they could dig up the chalk. The rent stayed fixed until the tenancy agreement was broken between my father and Blue Circle. A lot of that land has gone into chalk pits now and a lot of marshes down here which supplied the clay were dug up — they had floating pontoons down there and with these pontoons they then piped it, in slurry form, to the cement factory.

There were a few places where they only had a few feet of clay but they kept putting up these pontoons at a rate of knots so they could walk over the marsh to dig it. They must have taken a thousand acres over twenty five years. In some cases there was more topsoil than there was clay. That's still down there now and they are filling the pits up again now. They are going to make it into a nature conservation area - it was never filled in properly, it hasn't been properly drained, so it wouldn't make good farm land.

My father was an aggressive sort of farmer I think. We had sheep and dairy, plus beef, grew wheat and did a certain amount of gardening and went up to Covent Garden with peas and spring greens and those sorts of things when there was a market for it.

In 1960 he took over another farm at Tonbridge, a beautiful farm which ran down to the West Kent Fox Hounds Kennels. He let his nephew run it but things went wrong. I think communications were too far away. That only lasted for 7 or 8 years – they had a dairy herd down there.

I came into farming when I left school. I was too thick to do much else like going to university or anything. I always remember I had a school report at Sutton Valance when the master had made a few derogatory remarks, so I left school and I came onto the farm and I learnt about cows from Harry Stevens and just gradually developed. I wasn't too sharp at farming really.

You were expected to help out from the age of about 10, so I'd always been on the farm, just generally helping out. It was part and parcel of being a son on a farm. You just felt you were being useful.

I went into partnership with my father before I got married in 1966 – my brothers came in 8 or 10 years later and then we split the farm with my father having 51% share in each side – my two brothers on one side, me on the other. When my father could see everything was going all right, after 2 or 3 years, he backed away.

My brothers were Robert and John – they farmed the dairy farm at Court Sole – we only packed up doing dairy down there about 3 months ago (1997). The dairy side of the farm had lasted about 100 years. It's gone now, all economics, milk quotas. I think the land is not suited to cattle when you try and graze 2 or 3 to the acre. It is marsh ground and though we irrigated and reseeded, the proper grass growing areas are on the uplands and they well out yield this land twice over on grass.

In dry summers, despite irrigation, it is not the right ground for them. Economics has just driven dairy farmers out and, without being too critical of them, they should have expanded 15 or 20 years ago because the wages a herdsman gets is gradually getting more, he needed to be milking 100 to 120 – not the 80 or 90 cows they had. My theory is an extra 30 cows would have paid the herdsman's wages.

They're doing beef down there now and they've expanded a bit on the vegetable side but I don't know exactly what he'll do now the cows have gone. About 20 or 30 years ago a great friend of mine, Martin Gedney, was the first person in Europe to grow Iceberg lettuce; he got the seed in America and asked me to grow them for him. We were pretty unsuccessful for a couple of years. It was a new variety and we didn't know how to treat them, but we decided to go for one more year on it and we had an abundance that year – about 20 or 30 acres of them.

Then I started growing salad onions, and they've been a big income earner and then I got Marks and Spencer's interested in them and I was the only grower of them until about 10 years ago. There is a considerable acreage of them now but I'm still the only supplier to Marks and Spencer's. I developed a harvester for them – its got hydro-electrics and all sorts of funny things like that – I had a lot of help from a very good engineer.

We used to belong to Kent Veg. but in the last year we backed away from them and six of us have set up our own producer organisation; the Castles, myself, the brothers and the Batchelor's and we have an Egyptian with us, Henna, outside Cairo, he produces all the onions and beans for us in the winter months. We are in our first year so we are waiting to see how it goes, but it's kicked off well.

Richard the Ace Hunter:

Once when we were shooting by the sea wall, someone walking the other side of the wall put his head up and I thought it was a hare – I nearly shot him!

Luckily I am the most useless shot. If anything came over and I shot it, it was a bit of luck. Tim Long had a shoot coming up, so I though I'd better get down to Greenfield's at Canterbury and learn a bit more about shooting technique. I started firing clays and very little happened – then the instructor put a patch over one eye and I carried on shooting and some of the clays began falling out of the sky. The instructor advised me to keep the patch and to have a butt on the gun – which I didn't.

I went to Tim Long's and missed mostly everything all day and we got up to a drive just before lunch. I was positioned on the marshes, in the thickets running down with Marshland Farm. I was definitely a backstop gun. All the main guns were on the upland bit, fifty yards away behind the thicket, and the odd birds they missed because they got up in such a hurry would come over me on the marsh. I put the gun in the air and put the patch on and one or two of the birds came down. Tim Long was amazed and I was cock-a-hoop because I'd never done anything like that before.

We then went back to the farm yard for lunch and I felt someone scraping me on the shoulder. I asked what they were doing and they said they were scraping the parrot droppings off my shoulder – I still had the eye patch on and I looked like Long John Silver!

On another occasion – over at Batchelor's, in conjunction with Tim Long, all the guns were lying round a field and I was in some Brussels sprouts. The area was about

400yards long and 60 or 70 yards wide – they were coming through and right at the other end, about 400 yards away, someone shouted,

'Hare coming up!'

I was standing at the other end of the trackway and saw the hare running up it. It was sprouts one side and open fields the other so everyone could see what was happening.

The hare was coming towards me and they kept shouting, 'Hare coming up' so I let off a shot and nothing happened. The hare kept on coming so I let off another shot and still nothing happened. It went straight through my legs as I was trying to reload the gun. I had two more shots at it as it sped off into the distance and still nothing happened and one of the beaters said to me,

'All you had to do was kick it.'

Homeguard.

There was a chap called Old Martin, who died about ten years ago, he had worked for us on the farm. He was about my father's age and in the war he was in the Defence Army *(Home Guard)* and he was seconded to the medical brigade and there was a cinema in Cliffe Village down on the crossroads and that was the Medical Centre. They had to pretend that a bomber had come down and there was a pilot injured and they had to commandeer a vehicle to get him. It was 7pm and it was dark and in the winter and there would be a person who was pretending to be injured and they had to get him back to the medical centre.

Old Martin and a chap called Ken Smith heard the alarm go – Plane Down, and improvised. They requisitioned Henry Cousins van, who was the local undertaker, which had three feet of room and doors which closed on the back. It had a roof rack on the top, which the undertaker, who was a builder as well, would put his ladder on.

They went to Gatton's farm and there was the so-called injured person, Bob Francis, so they told him to lay down to be put on the stretcher. He didn't like it, but they put him on the stretcher and stuffed him in the back of the van with the doors flapping, but Bob was worried he was going to fall out so they decided to improvise. They strapped him firmer on the stretcher and put him on the roof rack. Well, coming back from Gatton's there is a series of five 90 degree bends, and they sped back to the cinema, nonchalantly got out of the van, only to find that Bob was not on top.

They retraced their steps and there was no sign of Bob anywhere and they got really upset about it. There was a general search by about 10 people but they could not find Bob Francis anywhere and the search was called off at 10.30 to be resumed at dawn.

One of the searchers dropped in to the Evening Star pub afterwards and there was Bob Francis, definitely the worse for wear! He had come off on one of the corners and fallen into a thicket of green elms and landed there, strapped to his stretcher, and rolled down the bank. Bob had thought, 'Blow this, I'm going home.' He just dropped in the pub to tell the story of these useless people! They had an enquiry about it – it turned out they had strapped him to the stretcher all right but they hadn't strapped him to the roof rack!

Foreign Travels

There was another story about the time Martin Gedney and I decided we would go out to Portugal and grow onions out there in 1985. On our first visit we met a Farmer named Joseph on a road between Toviro and Faro. We had a sketch map of the driveway to his house and arrived in Faro, picked up the hire car and went driving round the byways looking for something similar to the sketch. We weren't sure, they all looked similar – there was a stone wall on one side, olive orchards on the other, quite a large house – so we went up to the front door. As luck would have it there was a large dog on a chain just short enough so the dog didn't tear us to pieces.

We went round the farm and there were some women working about 200 yards away in a field – the sun was beating down on us and so far we hadn't had to use any Portuguese. Not that we knew any but we had a phrase book and Joseph could speak English. Martin was tall and had a craggy goatee beard and could pass for an Italian really.

Martin had lost the toss so he had to do the talking;

'Senor Setero, livo hero?'

I started laughing and the women went into a huddle and murmured amongst themselves so Martin said it again, then he said to me,

'They are completely ignorant peasants and don't understand a thing I am saying!'

With that one stood up, she was quite attractive, about 24 years old and Martin looked her straight in the eye and said, thinking she couldn't understand him,

'I could take you behind that wall and do something evil with you' and she replied, in perfect English

'Why are you so crude?'

I nearly fell over the wall laughing and it turned out she had been over to Kent Veg several times. We took her out to dinner that evening and asked her why they didn't answer when we asked them first time – she said,

'We didn't know who you were, we thought you were a Portuguese drunk or an Arab Butcher'

We had several years out there and it was quite a pleasant way of losing money I suppose.

Bob Macdonald

On Medicine, Mosquitoes and Malaria on the
Marshes.

Dr. Wall used to hold his surgeries in the Cock Pub in Grain – he'd see his patients and have a whisky. I got on quite well with him. Dr. Tilley didn't though. When Dr. Wall was old he wasn't doing very much and his patients would go along to Dr. Tilley's surgery and he would treat them – but he wouldn't take them on as a family because that would cut Dr. Walls income. When I said,

'This is wrong – you're treating them (and in those days they brought in a shilling prescription charge) and what's going to happen if Dr. Wall dies? You're going to be left with a nucleus of patients and someone will come along and set themselves up in competition, so you must take them onto your list.' But Tilley wouldn't do it and I was so cross I went to Dr. Wall and said,

'Look here, Tilley is doing all this for you, I want you to undertake that if you do retire you can sign them over to him before you do'.

There were two practices and they lived next door to each other. There had been Dr. Wall's practice and Dr. Morgan's practice – he was an Australian and had quite a big practice. Dr. Wall lived in an old institute which is now a housing estate. Morgan and Wall hadn't been the best of friends and when Tilley bought the practise, as you could in those days, Tilley was quite young and active whereas Wall was pretty ancient. Wall said he had to retire because Tilley had reported him for not doing any work, but this was totally untrue.

The reason was the executive council found out that we were collecting those shilling prescriptions charges and every quarter we would send to the executive council about £90 or £100 in shillings we had collected. Old Wall would send them 2/6d if he felt like it. It was typical of Dr. Wall who would say he would give them 4 bob if he felt like it.

He was the Home Guard Doctor during the war. He was an ex-military man and he would treat their pitchfork wounds and so on, but he didn't have a car as everything was restricted. I remember Bradford telling me once that on the day of a big inspection when the Brigadier was coming down, Dr. Wall as Medical Officer had to be there as well,

Dr Wall

so they sent a car for him. As he had a car and a driver he did a tour of the pubs and never did get to parade and nearly caused a riot because he'd gone off in this car. He was a real old character, and he didn't stand fools gladly. In fact I got on quite well with him.

And you know, when he did die he HAD signed his patients over to Tilley.

I don't think it's true that Dr. Wall didn't get on with Nurse Leaman. Nurse Leaman was a very good Christian, God fearing and upright lady and I think Dr. Wall was a bit of a rogue in his way. He was a very good doctor and patients loved him. I went to see a lady once and she said –

'Look at this stiff knee – that was Dr. Wall – he operated on the kitchen table'

I said ' Madam, he cured you of TB but I wouldn't have had the nerve to do anything like that'

He probably saved her life. He had opened up a TB abscess on the knee and as a result she got a stiff knee but he had cured the knee.

Dr. Wall was bankrupt. He looked after his patients. He was always immaculate. He had a big old Italian car and one of the refinery lorries hit him one day going down Coppers Green Road and they had to get a new one. I knew him when he was older. Nowadays there aren't the characters in the doctors. I think the change was when we got antibiotics.

I remember we had a great respect for the old doctors and we were frightened to death of them. I remember when I had measles we wouldn't stay in bed but you quickly got into bed when you saw a doctor's car coming. With the advent of antibiotics they just say, have a few pills and come back and see me. A lot of the mystique of doctors disappeared.

When antibiotics first came out I was in the Navy. I was the medical officer for the fishing protection fleet and we used to go to Norway and Sweden and there were only a few officers on the ship and when we went to a foreign port we would get invitation from ashore for the Captain, four officers and a doctor to go to dinner. At the end of the dinner I would be chatted up by a high official and they

Opening of new surgery at Hoo: Chris Rigby, Mary Moore and Bob Macdonald are on the right.

would ask me for penicillin for gingivitis. We were the only ship with penicillin and I don't know what he had but it certainly wasn't gingivitis, and I didn't like to ask.

At the next port the same thing would happen. In the end it got a bit silly, so I went to the Captain and told him what was happening. He didn't have much confidence in me and said he couldn't understand why they kept chatting to me. I explained they didn't have any penicillin there and he said, 'That's all right, we're on a goodwill mission – so long as we've got enough to get us back to England, that's fair enough'.

So I happily went on until at one port in Norway I was approached in the usual way and I said we didn't have any penicillin. He asked me to write him a prescription but I said I couldn't because I was from England so he asked me to put it in a diplomatic bag and send it from London.

I remember a Petty officer coming home and he had gonorrhoea for the fifth time and he told me penicillin was no good. I told him not to be silly, he just kept getting re-infected. He looked at me and he said ' Perhaps you're right, that's just life in general. I'm a fair martyr to it so just give me some more penicillin'

I did wonder if that's what all those High Officials wanted it for.

In the old days there was a lot of Malaria, though in those days they didn't know what it was. They called it the Ague. In the First War the survivors of Gallipoli were based at Sheerness when they came home and a lot of them had malaria, and they had a camp of recruits at Grain, and these recruits were getting malaria and they couldn't understand it. It was because in the summer the old veterans would come across to Grain and be bitten by the local mosquitoes who would then bite the recruits who would then get malaria.

In the last war we didn't have any, but it is still possible for the local malaria carrying mosquito to live. The last cases were in 1921 but there was a case in 1949 because the tankers were coming in. The last one was recorded by Donald Ross. It was because before the first war all the inhabitants had a midden in the garden or a stable outside where the pigs would be and that would be an ideal habitat for the malaria parasite.

When they did a survey they sprayed and found a thousand mosquitoes in one roof and they were the ones that were causing the ague as they called it then. When the refinery came they sprayed the marshes and got rid of them but the mosquito which causes the big bites and blisters aren't the malarial mosquitoes, they were marsh mosquitoes. The malarial mosquito is an innocent little lady unless she carries malaria and then she's fatal.

They did another survey in 1968 or so and they found there were just a few of these mosquitoes around and they had resisted the pesticides to destroy them.

About the time Dr Wall was going round canvassing to go on to the council everyone was complaining about the malaria and a lot of people were getting an intermittent fever so I approached Strood Council and they said it wasn't malaria – it was sand fly fever from when they build the power station at Grain. The Dutch had bought a lot of sand and it came from there and it was a very warm summer, so they sprayed the marshes again and it disappeared.

The malaria was always endemic.

By the end of 1918 50% of the local population of Grain had acquired malaria. It wiped out whole hamlets – it practically wiped the Comfort family out.

From 1850 to 1912 Stoke was very important because of the blue clay they took out for cement, and the gangs of muddies which comprised 5 men and a calorman, the man who took the turf off. They could earn quite a lot of money for a days work and they spent it up the pubs! They dug the clay out and at night they would use a thing called a blizzy-light, like a watering can, weak in the front and powerful behind, to light along the paths. It was quite an important time for the area and mosquitoes didn't seem to bother them – though they were certainly there.

I bought The Saltings in 1977. During the war there was supposed to have been a spy who blew up a ship and was executed at Sheerness Dockyard, though whether they got the right man or not I don't know. The sailors hung their hats on the side of the ship the night before and when it blew up all the hats blew across the Saltings. You could walk across the Saltings in those days. Allhallows and Grain were very small then and Stoke was the centre then and the Saltings were where people went to walk.

There was a salt shepherd on the Saltings and he said the ship was ablaze with light when it blew up and all the sailors had hung their washing and hats on the rail and he saw them all floating about on the Saltings.

In 1977 there was a rubbish strike and they piled all the rubbish there, but the plans were that they were going to build septic tanks and sewage stuff and I thought that was horrendous. I didn't mind the controlled reclamation but at the time The Saltings weren't on the SSSI – or my bit that they wanted to put rubbish on wasn't - but it was nearby. All the environmentalists were up in arms and they stopped it. They were going to have a rubbish tip very near the gardens of Grain and it was going to be enormous, with lots of lorries in and out.

There was an enquiry about it and I went to present a case on asthma, and one person did a very well presented thesis on why they should destroy some of the environment and then a QC got up and crushed him. English Nature hadn't bothered to come so when it was my turn to give evidence I said I thought it was infamous that 7 miles down the road we have an enquiry on a site which was surrounded by the SSSI where it wasn't going to be supplied by lorries and wasn't going to be near any population and we had an environmentalist against it.

Asthma cases are quite high here as it is one of the most polluted areas in the South of England and when they were going to put incinerators at Kingsnorth, Cuxton and Kelmsley, for 10 months they studied the effects. They assured me the effects of modern incinerators are quite harmless but they haven't assured me about the dioxins that come out to which there is no tolerance whatsoever.

They have now turned it down at Kingsnorth. I am President of the Men of Kent and presented my argument for them. Men of Kent are East of the Medway and Kentish Men are West of the Medway.

David and Barbara Dann of Hoo

On the Village Shop, School Mistress, Homeguard and Sailing.

David and Barbara Dann

My grandfather bought the business at Hoo Post Office and the Grovers, the old red brick place which is now an Indian Restaurant, in about 1903 and my father took it on when he died. Then we sold it out to the Co-op during the Second World War.

They made a good offer and even in those days small business were declining and there were three other businesses in the village and I don't think I was terribly interested in going into it.

There was Gough, who had a grocers shop and the Crescent Stores up the road – a man called Samms ran a grocers business where the Nat West bank is now. It was very old fashioned – everybody wore white shops aprons.

I vaguely remember the shop – Provisions – there was bacon, butter and lard sold on the right hand side, and grocery, mostly dried good – sugar, carrots and flour were sold on the left.

They served the whole village – farmers and landowners down to the ordinary people in the village. They had a delivery service and you could get credit.

When the Co-op took over it was the decay of the small business in the village – it was the start of its run down. It was too near the Medway Towns and too near London. It was neither village not town. – though officially Hoo is a village.

I didn't really go in the shop as a boy. I used to go in for messages and things like that but I wasn't allowed in, as it was a very formally run place. My father didn't want me in there and I didn't particularly want to go in there.

We used to have a doctor, Dr. Wall, who was drunk most of the time, and who once went to see a man and certified him dead, only to see him walking about later on. He was quite a famous sight in his Wolsely car and he often used to hold his surgeries in the pub.

Dr. Morgan invented a settling medicine for upset stomachs - it was kaolin and morphine. He lived at the Elms, which is now a nursing Home. He also sold brown jollop as a tonic for coughs and colds and that sort of thing.

My father was a great gardener, great Churchman and he loved the village. He was Hoo churchwarden from 1933 until he died in 1962. He started a lovely garden. He was born in Gillingham, and when they moved to Hoo he lived over the shop and in 1932, the year he was married, he built a house beyond my grandfather's house. It was called Lindor because there was a fashion in those days to put your two names together to name the house; Linton and Dora is Lindor.

My mother's father was Richard Knight. Knight's Road was named after him. He was a schoolmaster where

Yew Tree Lodge is. He was rather stern, rather severe, and rather forbidding. He wore a top hat and frock coat more or less to his last day. He retired in 1937 and built the house called Linton up on the top road, the last house on the right by Fourwents. My step-grandmother let us have it on lease for a wedding present.

When mother and father were married the school bell was rung formally at the wedding. My father was a very high churchman and they were married with a full communion service at 8 o'clock in the morning and they had a wedding breakfast at 9 a.m. in the school. The school was closed for the day and the bell was rung. My grandfather and grandmother both taught in the village school. It was run by the county council, set up under the 1894 Education Act. My mother became a school teacher too.

My mother went to Gravesend High School for Girls, now Gravesend Grammar School and she went to Bedford College in London and read History. After her degree she did a teaching diploma. She was one of the first women to ever do that sort of thing. She lived in for her second year and came home and lived in School House for her third when my grandmother died —she used to walk across the fields from Yew Tree Lodge to Sharnel Street and catch the train to Gravesend and change trains there for London, do her day's study and then come all the way back again.

After her mother died she was also running the house and looking after her three younger brothers. She was in the third year of her degree course then. If her mother hadn't died she would have gone on to teach history somewhere else.

My mother was a school teacher; during the war she did supply teaching. She became headmistress in 1946 or 47. She taught in Tovil, Snodland and round the whole of North Kent – she was a very much loved school mistress.

It was my mother who got me interested in history, reading and talking – the house was full of history books. I read History at Oxford.

I met my wife at Upnor. She started sailing at the age of two, but I didn't start until I was fourteen. My son won the Edinburgh Cup in the British National Dragon Championships in Torquay.

Mrs. Dann: When I first came down in 1947 we had a little dinghy, which we kept on a buoy at Rochester, and a man called Eakin, who was a Freeman on the river, rowed us out to it. A freeman has certain rights of landing and catching fish on the Medway and things like that. You have to be born within the bounds of the city to be a Freeman. The Mayor of Rochester is the Admiral of the River and Processes every year down to the bounds of Sheerness. The Hodsons are Freemen.

The Medway Yacht Club was a wooden shed on the Esplanade. My father had sailed before the war and started again afterwards when he came home again. We bought the dinghy and we used to sail above the Bridge. We joined the yacht Club about the same time that the club built the premises down here. In 1947 or 48, it was bought by David Clarabut and Michael Wood, a family of estate agents in Rochester, they pioneered the younger generation. When they built the club, they rented half of it from APCM and a bit from Walter Brice . A friend of ours who was living in the area was the secretary of the Yacht Club and he had an exercise from the Engineers. The Yacht Club is built up on a sort of mound and the engineers built that mound so that the buildings could be built on it.

David Dann: My earliest memories were the LDV – Local Defence Volunteers – the Home Guard. My father was a lieutenant of the Home Guard. He ran the Hoo Platoon. His Commanding Officer for the Hoo Peninsular was Maurice Gill, the Uncle of David Clarabut, and he lived up on Shorne Ridgeway. There are still some of the old Pill boxes about.

The battle of Britain was fought above us and as children we used to go out and pick up bits of hot shell. We used to stand in the garden and cheer our pilots on. There was a very strange smell about shrapnel. We were very lucky, especially the dockyard, as there wasn't a lot of heavy bombing here.

I remember mostly the rations, and sleeping under the stairs in my blanket. We had an air raid shelter but we stayed under the stairs. My mother saw a Zeppelin come over and drop bombs on Cliffe during the first war – she was about 12 or 13 at the time, in 1916.

At Kingsnorth, by where the power station is, during the first war, I can remember just seeing the sheds, but it was what used to be an airship station. They were knocked down at the beginning of the Second World War in 1940-41. It used to be a naval Station and the airships came under the Navy in those days.

I remember there was a marker fence, which had firing trenches in case the enemy ever invaded Hoo, and my father had to be careful digging in the garden in case there was a bomb buried in the garden, which would have been used to throw at the enemy. The threat of invasion was very real then and they (the Home Guard) took their role very seriously. At first they met in the Windmill Public House, then it was bombed and the landlord died so they moved HQ to a house called St. Werburgh Lodge – opposite Bradford's garage, where the Killicks lived. It was a big fruit farm then.

There was a fire station round the back of St. Werburgh Crescent – people kept fire watch from the Church Tower.

Others who served in the Home Guard were Crawford, the Robertsons, Charlie Keats from Grain and a retired Grenadier Guards Sergeant major called Clegg who lived in Bells Lane. He took my father being in command very well really considering they were all amateurs. My father was too young for the first war and too old for the second. He was a reserved occupation because he ran the village shop.

Rationing affected everything. You just sold what you had got. My grandfather sold the shop to the Co-op on the proviso that my father stayed on, or else he would have gone to work for the big wholesaler in Maidstone.

Father kept geese and hens on our land. The house is called Cups House and the whole ground was called Cups Meadow and was owned by Styles and Winch the brewers who owned the Five Bells.

The Dray horses would unload at the Five Bells and then they would be turned out in the meadow here overnight. Then the land was no longer needed so it went to whoever owned the shop, a man called Chapman then.

My father stayed on at the Co-op and so they kept the customers - otherwise they would probably have gone somewhere else. My father would have liked to have been an artist – he was a very good sketcher and painter in an amateur fashion. He died at 62 of lung cancer and we then built this house to be near his Mother.

My grandfather, Y T Dann had photographs done and sold as postcards in the shop in the thirties. YT stands for Young Thomas. The Linton part of the name comes from the village of Linton near Maidstone – my grandfather started off using the name. There have been Danns in the records since 1420 something in either Linton or Boughton

Monchelsea or Marden – down in that part of the Weald. In the family tree most of the Dann's were shopkeepers or publicans or small farmers.

I was one of the first war time pupils in the junior part of the Kings School, Rochester – I was there for 10 years. I did a year at the school in the village then as my mother and grandparents were teaching there, I went to a convent in Frindsbury and then to the Kings School from 1942 to 1952. I did my National Service in the Navy until 1954 then I went to Oxford in 1954 until 1957. I read History.

When I went to Oxford I wanted to play rugby and be a school teacher but I went into Lloyds instead. I was an underwriter there. I handed over my syndicate to my deputy in 1990 and I became chairman of a Lloyd's Agency and the Deputy Chairman of the whole firm. It was a firm called Kilves, one of the biggest companies quoted at Lloyds. I did litigation and underwriting, I did the claims for a firm Aerols, run by Jill Castle's father until 1977, ran an aviation syndicate for 12 years, then became chairman of the Men's Agency which looked after the affairs of the individual members of Lloyds.

There are no more teachers in the family. The sailing is still in the family though – Peter got a blue for sailing at the university and Kate can still sail.

A lot of people came here from Wales in the fifties. The McLain's and the Robertson's came down from Scotland in the farming depression but we have a lot of Welsh in the village. They came from Aberfan to work at the Anglo Iranian Oil Co. and they built the Oil Refinery.

Hoo is changing and growing and the vicar is getting worried that we are running out of churchyard space

Marion Stopps of High Halstow born 1917

Sausages, parties and the Christmas round.

Marion and Arthur Stopps.

I lived in Stoke originally, went to the grammar school then met and married Arthur Stopps, a butcher; we had one daughter, Susan. We first lived in Hoo in a bungalow opposite the butcher's shop; then moved into the shop and lived over the business. It was a family business, Arthur's father came to Hoo from Bedlow in Buckinghamshire, they had a farm there. I think he went into Strood to start with, of course Roy would have known, Roy Stopps, he died last year. He used to copy his granddad, he thought a lot of him and of course they were good butchers, they did the job properly, and followed him with the family history. I don't know all of it, I married into it.

Arthur had the shop built in 1922. Before that he was at the shop which used to be on the opposite side of the road. He was there for quite a few years before he built the shop at 59 Stoke Road, which was just along the road from the Five Bells pub on the corner; the dentist's wife lives there now. The shop was closed in the 1970s.

There were two butchers' shops in Hoo at the time we lived at the shop, Broads and Stopps. We were in partnership with his brother George, who lived further along the road in the village with his family. We lived at the shop from just after the war started in 1940 until 1962 when they had a house built in Christmas Lane, High Halstow, it was the first new house built there. Arthur died in 1969.

I didn't work in the shop. Arthur opened the shop at 6am in the morning. At that time Berry Wiggins oil refinery was in operation nearby and it was amazing, before I was up in the morning, you would hear people calling out their orders as they cycled past to work, "Arthur, we want us so and so". They would call for their orders on the way back after work.

It was that sort of community, everyone knew everyone else, everyone knew each other's Christian names, it was very different altogether than now.

We used to go to Rochester market to buy all our stuff. Years ago, they used to drive the cattle to the marshes from Rochester market and leave them there until they were ready to go for slaughter. We had our own slaughterhouse at Stoke where they did all the slaughtering.

Arthur had a brother, Dennis, who had a shop in Stoke, the shop belonged originally to their father, and when he died, Arthur took on the Hoo shop, and Dennis the Stoke shop. Dennis' son Roy had the Stoke shop after.

The time when the cattle were driven back from Rochester or to the marshes was before Marion's time but it used to happen like that. In later years, the cattle were moved to Stoke from Rochester by cattle truck, but even then it was very hard work. They used to go on Mondays and Tuesday mornings to market, then go to Stoke at about 3:00pm in the afternoon to slaughter cattle and they would get back at 12 midnight.

In those days, at Christmas time, they would have to go to buy the chickens and turkeys, kill them, pluck them and prepare them for the table themselves. There were two people working for them at that time but the butchers did everything. Nowadays the poultry comes to the shops already prepared. It's like beef, you don't see sides of beef hanging in the butcher's shops as you used to, then if you wanted a piece of suet for Christmas, the butcher would cut a piece off the side of beef, now you would have a job to find any. Now you would just buy a packet, you couldn't get it in packets then, but people liked to buy it nice and fresh.

The older generation likes something, their meat, with the juice coming out. I had a piece of filet steak last night and really, it was nothing like it used to be. A fillet steak was really something special, you hardly had to cook it at all, but now it's a bit tough. And beef generally; you can't get a piece of beef like it used to be. Well, there is Wilkes at Cranbrook still, they were the ones who had the sausage recipe.

We were very well known for our sausages. People used to call at the shop when they were going on holiday and take a pile of sausages with them. They were known to be the best in Kent. Roy gave his recipe to Wilkes when he had to give up and some of the older people still ring up Wilkes when they want a good sausage; Wilkes make a certain amount to order. Their meat is good too.

The Dann's used to have a grocers shop, the old man, I can't remember him but I remember his son and his grandson, David who lives in Hoo. He didn't go into the grocery business. I don't really remember much about the shop. There was a baker's shop, Broad's, he was on the corner and Cuckoos, down Church Street in Hoo.

There was a baker's shop in Stoke, Joe Stone the Midnight Baker, yes, he used to come round at 9 0'clock at night. Of course I know more about Stoke because my grandfather was there and he owned some of the marshes and he used to sell clay to the Gillingham Cement works. The muddies used to come to the house on Friday night to be paid. We used to live at Coningsby and I remember they would come in and sit at the kitchen table with an oil lamp waiting to be paid. My grandfather was a dear old man, Mr. Wooley, Henry Wooley; he used to have barges down in the creek at Upper Stoke. And I always remember, he had a telescope, a good one, and he would sit in the window watching for the barges to come in.

Dr. MacDonald ended up with that telescope, he used to come and see my father and eventually my father told him he'd better have it. Only recently, Dr Mac told me - 'you know I've had a lot of use out of that telescope' - because, of course he had his sitting room upstairs and could use it there. Of course, it was a different sort of life then, my grandfather had a shoot and he had two sons and they used to go off shooting together, it was all different. A slower life, people used to take their time, and of course people never locked their doors at night. And at Christmas time, people would open their doors and would call you in for a drink if you were passing by.

The community was very different then. Halstow was a lovely village but of course it changed when BP came. We used to have a lot of pleasure with the tennis and the dances and the dinner-dances, then of course BP came and they built a lot of houses and its all different now. High Halstow people complained a lot, the BP people brought money to the community and it was different, if you have money life is different.

Before, even if you didn't have money, everyone was friendly, everyone knew everyone else. You played sport, you played tennis, everyone joined in. We played tennis after our daily jobs - we used to do the teas and we had a good tennis club. I still have the cups we won, Arthur and I, it was good fun. There was friendliness, whoever you met you'd stop and talk and have a jolly good laugh. There was so much laughter.

I can always remember at Christmas, Arthur used to serve Wainscott, Hoo, High Halstow, Stoke and Grain with meat and at Christmas, Arthur would go round and would come back, well - sloshed! He would start at Whitehall Farm not far from Hoo and there would be a large whisky on the table for him, this would be at about 7 o'clock in the morning. It would take all day to do this round, you'd call at the pubs and at nearly every house you called at there would be a drink.

When he came home he always arranged for the Hoo Silver Band to come outside the shop and play Christmas carols that was on Christmas Eve. Of course this happened every Christmas Eve and we used to give them mince pies and things and he'd stand there and the tears would be rolling down his face, he was still a little bit sloshed of course and we all used to laugh and get a bit emotional.

We lived in Coningsby Villa, a detached house, the last one before you went into Upper Stoke. Aunt Wynn, whatever her name was, had a bungalow, Maisy was the name of the bungalow, they lived just above us in Middle Stoke. She was very clean, I suppose she didn't want to dirty the house, so they didn't live in it, that's what we heard. They lived in the shed instead. She used to wear a white apron, she was a Mortley.

Then there were the Betts, he was a bit of a lad, and I remember when I was very young, if he used to meet me, he had a walking stick and he'd poke me in the middle and say 'and how are you my girl'. He was quite friendly, and I remember Ian's father, Philip, I'm talking about the older Bett, Robert Bett . And Mrs. Mortley, Ron Mortley's Mother, used to be his housekeeper. Phillip came, he was a young fellow about 18, and he had a sports car, nice looking chap. He didn't have good health but carried on farming and then his son Ian took over.

Now, who else have you got - Kitty Nash, Fred Muggeridge's second wife, was a schoolteacher, she was different to his first wife, she had things just about right. They got on together, I suppose, I don't really know..

There was Amy Harbour, she was a Muggeridge she was Jim Muggeridge's sister. She was the schoolteacher at the local school, the primary school in Stoke. She was very strict and used to have a funny way with her. I don't know, I suppose she was a good teacher. She married the wheelwright Bert Harbour. He was the undertaker as well.

My father was a squadron leader in the Airforce and when he retired from that he went into oil and storage and he was District Sales Manager there until he retired. He knew everyone in Stoke and when he used to be cutting the hedge, wearing his panama hat, he'd talk to everyone going by.

Of course, the Harbours used to have their place just opposite down the road, and father used to go down and talk to him. They used to make the coffins there at that time, now I think you more-or-less get them off the shelf. He made one coffin and he asked father if he'd go down to Grain with him and he had the coffin all loaded up on the trailer. I don't know if there was a body in it, but coming back along the

Grain road, the thing tipped over into the ditch, coffin and everything, it was a bit muddy in the ditch.

But Mr. Harbour used to go around with the trailer and with coffins on the back and do his business.

You see, horses and carts were all the go in those days and you needed a wheelwright for the carts and well, it was a very steady life then.

Jeff and Betty Mortley

The White Horse, Stoke, Muddies and Bashing up.

There was Mortley's in the Muddies. I don't think they used this pub much, I think they used the Lower Stoke and the Nag. Of course you always had the muddies of Hoo and the muddies at Stoke who used to have a bash up now and again. Meet up and have a good old ding dong. I suppose they had a ringleader on both sides. It was rivalry, like rivalry in sports – Hoo against Stoke, there was always a funny game going on. They used to get black eyes and goodness knows what! *(Jeff is laughing)* There's still rivalry everywhere isn't there – even between pubs when they play a game of bat and traps or darts. It might not end up in a brawl but the feeling is still there.

I've been at The White Horse for 27 years and before that it was Uncle Frank for 12 years and another Uncle Frank before him for 48 years – so that's 87 years and before that there was a Mortley married a Rainer , there was Rainer here before that – Bill Rainer. It's been in the hands of uncles for a long time.

It was a different life in those days, it was more-or-less a village community, It's not now, that's all changed.

You've got different people coming into the village. It's not their life. Community fellowship has gone. People come into the village now and look at you as if to say 'who the ruddy hell are you' and you've lived here all your life! It's passing trade now, they come by car, if I get 2 or 3 in from the village I'm lucky.

They still had a children's' room years ago, down where we play darts now. That was the children's room. We had a football team and a cricket team – which this village was a centre of. You know, you had your committee meetings here and years ago, you'd have an annual dinner in the pub. I've sat in there with 50 of us having a meal. The cricket team would organise it with the landlord.

The cricket field is ploughed up now. They don't play cricket at Hoo School now.

We had the Wing Commander, who has sadly passed away. He had an OBE for the Berlin airlift – apparently he bought a plane down in a field and saved lives. Something went wrong with the aircraft. Ron wasn't really home to talk about things like that and when he retired he went lecturing. Lovely chap Ron was. He worked for the Medway

Educational department to different schools, he interviewed school leavers to put them in the right direction for jobs.

My father he only worked for Medway Oil Storage company – all through his life, 'til the day he retired. He meant a hell of a lot to me. We done everything – the Mortleys – we had a cricket time amongst Uncles and the rest. We used to play local teams that wanted to play us. We played against Fenn – that was a regular event. We sought our own entertainment. Football, cricket darts, drinking. A wonderful village life.

My father wasn't much involved apart from coming for a knees up at the pub here when my great Uncles run it. He helped out now and then – it wasn't his life though. He did mostly Ship Work. My father used to come home to six of us, howling kids around him.

Betty comes in and offers tea and coffee; Doug introduces her as his babysitter from a hundred years ago!

Betty: You ought to talk to Phyllis Driver, I take Phyllis out – she's the one who tells me everything. She used to have the village shop.

Jeff: They started off in a little wooden hut in the front garden, just up by the meadow in the 1950's. The carrier services they were before the war , George Mortley ran that.

Betty: They used to put their groceries on the bus – The International did it.

Jeff: That was through Maidstone and District Office in Military Road Chatham. Mother would shop, put it into the office and they'd send out the shopping to her on the bus – she'd pick it up here. I think it was a favour for mum – they had a soft spot for her.

Betty: It was a better community when I was growing up, 30 years ago. I went to Stoke Primary. Mr. Godfrey lived next door – he was the headmaster, he was a lovely man. Took an interest in everyone and everything. He lived in the school house – he was a Victorian gentleman. Firm but fair. Had a club foot didn't he? He used to play cricket for us. If he was out around the village and saw you doing something you shouldn't he'd tell you off wouldn't he? But the Headmistress now at Stoke, she comes from Gravesend.- she's not in the community. I think it's so sad.

Jeff: If the vicar told you off, or the Headteacher, you'd respect them. But not these days.

Betty: Also there was the village Bobby then wasn't there. Mr. Wilson. Tub Wilson – Arthur Wilson. Rochester come through now, a woman. In those days the village policeman knew everybody.

Apparently in that first house, there was a chap called Bogey Russell and he had this beautiful Apple Tree and he was so fed up with the kids pinching from it that he chopped it down to spite the kids. But it wasn't vandalism – every child has scrumped an apple haven't they? I think people stood in awe of authority then.

I think Jeff and I were brought up – how can I say, my mother and father were just ordinary working people. I was brought up to respect authority. My mother was a Liverpudlian who worked for Mr. Marsh (Doug) for a long, long time. Cutting greens, picking up potatoes anything that was going.

Jeff; That's another thing – even when the women were pregnant they'd be out working on the farm.

Doug: *If Betty's sister were here, Ann, she'd tell you a story. It was so cold, and Anne was so cold, I picked her up*

Potato harvesting at Gattons

and wrapped her in a corn sack, took her into the barn Brick
House to get her warm, She was about three at years old.
On no – it was Edna! We warmed her up and she was fine.

Doug, Betty and Jeff have general chat about the old
village characters, Jeff' s rich laugh rolls out with the first
whisky of the day.

Betty: The brothers, Tom and Frank could have told
you a lot. About Tom getting his toe shot off in the war. We
always said he'd done it on purpose so he could come home

(*Betty laughs*) He was in France when it was shot off. There were three brothers, they never got on, they never married and they all lived together but never got on. Tom, Frank and Arthur – we used to call him Smiler. He was always smiling.

Then Tom died and left Arthur and Frank but they really didn't talk to each other, did they? Arthur came in one day and said ' Have you got any candles?' and I said '

'Why, are you expecting a power cut?' And he said, 'No, he's taken all the light bulbs out!'

Frank paid for the hire of the television so Arthur would have it on and be watching out the window for Frank coming back. He'd have to turn it off – but Frank would go up and feel it – make sure it wasn't warm!

Arthur came in and said ' I've lost my frying pan – can't find it anywhere' He looked everywhere for it and came in a few days later and said 'I've found it, Frank hid it under the bed'. That's just how they were. Wouldn't buy each other a drink.

Jeff: What about Aunt Wynn? Mrs. Gaskin, Aunt Win – Winifred May Mortley. She was a very thin, hard working, lovely woman. She was in her 30's when I was a tot. She used to have one of those bungalows along there, but she

111

never lived in the actual bungalow. They used to live in the shed. They had a wooden shed out the back and that's where they lived, two of them, her and her Mother. To keep the bungalow clean – and the furniture was wrapped up in paper, literally.

Betty: Do you remember just before we got married you said come on I'll take you round to Aunt Nell's – which was Wynn's Mum – she'd fallen and broken her hip – I think she was about 90. And Aunt Wynn had got her wrapped on the settee in newspaper to keep her warm!

They stayed in the shed. She cooked in the garage – had a primus stove out there. She used to wear an old sack for a pinny. She was like an old Victorian lady – black stocking, all dressed in black and her hair was all pinned. She died of malnutrition so they say. She has a load of food in the shed but died of malnutrition.

Jeff: Her husband would come home from Barry Wiggins at 5 o clock and start on the farm to do 2 hours overtime, half past five to half past seven. He used to roll his cigarettes like a matchstick – he was that tight. They were tight. Who was the old boy who used to sit outside when I used to go to school:

Doug: Bill Ostler – yes Bill Ostler, his grandfather walked from Somerset to Stoke looking for work.

Betty: Do you remember Bernie Johnson – he was a character – he couldn't read or write but he was a coalman, a wood contractor, refuse collector – emptied the toilets – the dry waste. He went to Canada when he was a young man and when he came back he built this ranch style house right opposite the school, down the gravel pit.

Jeff: How did grandma get mixed up with the windmill?

Doug: It was a Smith that was at the Windmill originally – Harry Smiths grandfather had it. He also had that cottage opposite because there is a plaque on that house, RBS with the date on it, 1780, something like that.

Jeff: I wonder – because I know my grandmother rode from the Windmill to Hoo Church on a horse to get married. That was my grandmother. The groom was most likely flat out in a cart behind!

Jeff: What about old Mo Muggeridge - there's a character! He used to ride a bike round to his farm and his missus used to walk along! And there was an Austin 7 in the garage that they never got out!

Betty: He was a very rich farmer and when he died, I know this is true, his wife went into the post office and asked for a refund on her television license because she could no longer afford it. He left all his money to cats and dogs.

Doug: Yes he made sure none of his family got anything. Hated them. There was a family feud. Even his wife,

Betty: She was a midwife – tiny lady and he was a great big tall man.

Jeff: It's like Phyllis, will tell you more about the history of the pub than I can. This is not the original pub – that was burnt down, it was a wooden one, it was further along the road here . From there they went to the Square which was a few houses across the road – and from there to here.

Where ever there's a church there seems to be a pub

Doug: Yes because they'd live in the pub while they built the church.

Betty: In the Church at All Hallows, the altar now, it was the original altar that had gone into the Rose and Crown. They've got it back and it's been graffiti on it – you know what it's like in the pub, they scratch their names on it. Well, they've taken it back into the church as the written on Altar. Don't know how it got into the Rose and Crown.

MABEL DANPURE and PAULINE LEWIS

Sitting around a tiny kitchen table, we talk about being in service, falling in love, the war and squatting in huts.

Mabel: I was in service in Bromley. A lady used to live in Upper Stoke and we were friends with people in Stoke. Dad would go to the pub and we would go and see this friend and have a little get together in the house. One day her niece was there and this friend Cheeseman was there ironing a maid's uniform. I didn't want to go on the fields, so I told my mum I wanted to go out and not stay round here and a few months later we had a letter from Bromley saying that they wanted a general (that's what it was called) and would I be willing to come up for an interview.

I had just turned fourteen when I left school. I thought I would like to go, but mum couldn't read or write, or only very little because she left school at twelve.

I went for the interview and they were both doctors, and she was expecting her second child. It was like a college really, you took a course in everything and I didn't know whether I was going to like it or not really, but I went and I told all my friends if I was paid a week I would stop a week and if I was paid a month I would stop a month. When the week had gone by I didn't know if I liked it or not so I went on for a fortnight, and thought I would like it so I stayed. I was there for eighteen years, and I still hear from them now, from Mrs. Adamson, though he's died.

They were very nice people though when I first went in I somehow got the impression that a man I saw through a window was the gardener. After I'd seen mum on the train the lady said "I think we'll start as we mean to go on, Mabel" so I went up and put my black and white uniform on then and a blue and white in the morning, and she told me about working at the table.

I knew a bit because I'd read quite a lot about dishing things up, but when I went into the dining room who should be sitting at the other end of the room but the man I took to be the gardener - he was the boss. I spoke to him about it when I got to know him better.

The first six months or so I used to find a sixpence or a shilling or a penny lying anywhere when I was cleaning and I got so fed up I said "If I find any more money lying about Madam, I'm going to keep it" She said "Fair enough Mabel, that's how I test an honest person." She had been putting it down deliberately. She said she could always tell if a person was clean by when they came for an interview and at some point they would get a handkerchief out, and she could see if it was clean.

Until just before the war broke out I was the only girl living in the house. The gentleman doctor, Dr. Thomas, went to Great Ormond Street and he was very friendly with another doctor and they got transferred to this big house which had twenty five rooms. There they had two gardeners, two daily ladies who used to clean, and a parlourmaid (I was under-parlourmaid then) a cook and Miss Thornton who was the doctors' secretary and another lady who was German who was trying to learn English. She had to go back when war broke out.

I stayed there on my own for about six months because the doctor was up in London all the time at the hospital and he said he thought he was paying me unnecessarily and he would have to put the house in storage, so that was when I came back to Allhallows.

I lived with dad till I was fourteen and when I got back from Bromley I came to live with mum for a little while and then I went to work at Lodge Hill.

I met my husband in a greengrocers shop in Bromley when I was about fifteen. He was just a friend then and I had others, but after I came back to live in Brick House I stayed working at Lodge Hill for two and a half years and then I was expecting Victor, my son, and that was when I lived at Brick House with my mum until my husband was de-mobbed.

He went to North Africa in the war. He was moved from pillar to post because he was in the Pioneers. He couldn't see very well but it was a unit which prepared the way for the other units to go in, though I didn't know that till afterwards, and he was there nearly all the time. We only had letters every now and again. He was in the Royal Engineers. He didn't like to talk about the food when he came back and he was a bit choosy about what he ate, like his brother who was a prisoner of war all the time in Spandau in Germany.

After my husband came back we lived with mother for about six months or a year because there wasn't much room in Brick House for two families because my sister was living there as well. There was an army camp at Allhallows and there were twenty five ladies with families who decided to go into the huts and squat. They broke into them because the camp had been disbanded. This happened all over the country.

I had the biggest hut on the camp because no-one else wanted it. One person went in and started to scrub and did a bit the size of a table and left it, it was such hard work, and a lady called Mrs. Fritter phoned me up and said there was one hut going, would I like it and I said yes, because we had a family.

It was pouring hard with rain when we went down to the camp and we were there six months before we moved in, painting and whatever and then the council realized that people were determined to have these houses so they put kitchens and sinks in to make them more habitable. So then we stayed there and we were there just over five years. They said five years and then we've been here ever since. People were so desperate for housing and you couldn't get a house anywhere. We didn't have the money to buy anything.

Pauline: I lived in a hut as well, in Cambridge, because there was nowhere else you could go.

Doug: Then they built pre-fabricated houses, didn't they, all round the country.

Pauline: They were supposed to be a temporary measure but they're still about. In Cambridge they built bricks round them. They were quite nice really.

I was born in Cambridge and my parents lived there. I came here to visit my aunt and one year I came down, in 1946, and my husband, as he was to be, had wheedled my cousin to meet me off the train, and he was in the Fleet Air Arm, and in uniform, and I fell in love with him straight away and we were married in Cambridge, but my husband used to work at Shorts Aircraft place on the Esplanade in Rochester where they made seaplanes.

When he was called up he was on an aircraft carrier but when he was de-mobbed Shorts had left and gone to Ireland so there wasn't very much work. After he left the Navy he was out of work for about eight months then just before we got married he went to Cambridge and he worked for Marshall's Airport. He was a coach and body builder. He used to build cattle trucks and television vans and things like that. That was when TV first started taking off.

We lived in Cambridge for nine years and I had three children. Marilyn was the eldest, then my son Alan, and Diane was the youngest. For the first three years of our marriage we lived with my parents, like Mabel did. I had two children quite quickly, so in the bedroom there was a single bed, a double bed and a cot. My father worked on the railway and was on the night shift, so you can tell it wasn't very comfortable at times.

I used to go and worry the Cambridge Council Housing department about somewhere to live and almost three minutes walk from the town centre, there was a camp where the ATS had been stationed during the war and there were these half brick and half wood huts. They were quite attractive to look at and they made them into two bedrooms and a huge sitting room and outside there was a corridor going across.

In the corridor there was a shed, a coalbunker, a sink and toilet and a little room where there were two boilers to do the washing. I thought that was marvelous. I was offered one of these because I had been worrying the council every day. My parents lived about three miles outside Cambridge. We moved into the hut and we had it for three years and then we moved to Cherry Hinton village where I was given a house.

Then my mother-in-law was taken ill and the four boys had a conference about what would happen to Dad who by now was eighty years old and was getting around very well, but he needed looking after and they decided that he would come and live for a year at a time with each of the boys. Well, one lived in Enfield, one lived in Gravesend, one at High Halstow and at the time we were living in Basildon New Town.

When mum died there was another conference and this was suggested. I didn't say anything at the time, I just sat there as I was only a daughter in law and then they started asking their wives what they wanted to do.

Frank lived in Enfield, but both he and his wife had good jobs and their children had just started to go to the Grammar School, so they didn't want dad, because dad was incontinent as well and their toilet was upstairs. Wilf had got a building business in Gravesend and he was settled and his wife didn't particularly want to give her home up and come to Stoke. John and Glad, who lived in High Halstow, didn't want to come back and live in the cottage, so that left Ray and I and three children in Basildon.

I always knew my husband wanted to come back this way, he loved Lower Stoke and the village, though our address was actually Allhallows in those days and when they said to me about Dad selling up and coming to live a year with each of us and asked me what I thought about it I said that would be the quickest way to kill him. I asked how could a man who had lived out in the country all these years possibly cope with a modern house. We all had upstairs toilets.

When my father needed the toilet he couldn't always make it and he used to use the shed in the garden because that was quicker than anything. When we came to tell dad what we suggested he blew up and refused to move, so I said to my husband that we would come and live with him.

I left a beautiful modern house in Basildon to come to a cottage, which had just cold water, and an ugly big sink four inches deep in the kitchen, and a bucket toilet up the garden. Once you have had all the mod cons it did come as a bit of a shock. I used to hate that toilet up the garden. That's how we came back. We were only here from September 1957 and in 1958 they put main drainage in so we had a toilet put in by the side of the house so that was better. Then I had a long kitchen because it was two kitchens made into one and up at one end my husband partitioned it off and made it into a bathroom and we had a six foot bath and a "Saviour", a ten gallon water heater there. Then I was able to wash Dad in the bath quite often then, even if he didn't like it much.

When we first came back in the September, my husband tried to get a job at the oil refinery at Grain, but he couldn't be taken on until the February. We couldn't live without any wages coming in, so he went out doing the same kind of woodwork as before, only he made portable school rooms and things like that for a firm in Wainscott, until he went to the oil refinery on 4th February 1958 and he worked there till he died in 1979.

I worked for seven years at the village school, Stoke Primary, as school secretary. Mr. Morris was the head when I started and Mr. English came after that. My children went there. My daughter was ten when we moved here and my son nine, so they were there a short time before going to

Hundred of Hoo School but my youngest daughter started school there. Marilyn still lives in the village, and has been married for thirty one years, my son is in Adelaide, Australia, and my youngest daughter is in Walderslade. She has three children and a granddaughter.

Mabel: My daughter Sylvia lives in Gainsborough; she's a churchwarden there and has two boys. My son lives in Sheerness and is a long distance lorry driver and has a family of four. He started in the Merchant Navy. He loves the water. We hardly ever see the sea. When we were younger and lived at Brick House we used to walk to the sea and never think anything of it. Later they used to have a speed bike dirt track there, before the war. They used to have a speedboat going from Allhallows over to Southend. We used to go in the morning and come back on the tide in the evening.

Pauline: When we lived in Basildon, our main shopping centre was Southend and there used to be a little man standing on the front and advertising a day trip over to Allhallows, though we never did it because it would have taken all our spare time to walk to Stoke and back to get the boat again.

Mabel: When you look back there's quite a lot to look back on.

Pauline: There used to be Old Yonk, and all sorts of nicknames. I used to hear the older villagers talking about these weird people, Stumpy Watson, who had a wooden leg, Peeler Bradley, Ginger and Dido Hammond, Dig Walker. Old Mr. Thomas was the old junk man and when he was in the pub he used to sing an old song called "Why does the winkle always turn to the right?" when he was quite inebriated and do all the actions.

Doug: There was old Bert Thomas and Con Saville who would keep you in fits of laughter after he'd had a few.

Pauline: Fred Osbome used to play the spoons and was said to be terrific at it.

Mabel: He was, and you never saw him without a buttonhole. He loved the flowers.

Pauline: He would sit on the cart when he worked for Muggeridge's and he used to slump so low I thought he was asleep and thought the pony knew where to take him. He wasn't really asleep. He never said much, just grunt, but he was hilarious in the pub. He was quite a dry old stick.

Mabel: There was old Jimmy King. He used to sell peanuts and rhubarb.

Pauline: Stumpy Watson used to play the drums in a little band they had got up for a fete originally, They formed up outside the Nags Head and marched along and they used to go up by the Methodist church and Stumpy went the other way because he couldn't see over the drum. I'm the last Plewis living in the village.

My sister in law, Joy Plewis, used to live in the village but moved to Broadstone with two friends – she had her ashes put in her parents' grave though. I was pleased because she had done an awful lot for the village. She was eighty one when she died. She used to play the organ at the chapel and she was school secretary in Mr. Godfrey's time. She belonged to the tennis club and organized a lot there and she did a lot for the chapel. She ran the Sunday school for the children. When June came to teach at the school she started up a Guide and Brownie pack and Joy used to help with that and we used to go country dancing all over the place.

When we started the country dancing we were about twenty two ladies. None of our husbands would come. We danced and all the ladies taking the men's part wore a blue band. We went to a great big country dance at Chatham Town Hall and there were three large circles of people, all men and women. We of course knew who were the "men" in our section, but when you got parted and went round, the other dancers got a bit confused because two ladies had suddenly appeared and they didn't know that one of them was supposed to be a man.

One of our characters of the village, Ivy, who used to keep the Ship, changed sex about four times in this circle and caused havoc. Suddenly it all came to a grinding halt and nobody knew who was who. In the end the caller made us sit down. Ivy said loudly as we went to sit down "Well, that was good, wasn't it, - did you enjoy it?" We all said yes and she said, "All I came for really was my fish and chip supper."

I will never understand why people say that village life is dull, because if you join in village life it is never dull. We've had some wonderful times. I would never have had such experiences had I stayed in Cambridge or Basildon. When we used to go into the village you used to speak to everyone. It would take me two hours to get there and back. Now everybody jumps into a car. In the Post Office queue the other day a young girl was complaining of being bored in the village and I told her I have been here for forty one years and have never been bored. It must be a different attitude.

We learnt lots of crafts in the W.I., rush work, train work, we made eiderdowns, glove work, and made lampshades. We were both in the W.I. When I first came here I was told my mother-in-law was a keen W.I. member and as she was no longer here I was to take her place. So I went to W.I. and I thought it was the most boring thing.

I went during a meeting and because I was poorly I wasn't able to go again until the following June. I went then and there was a lady there talking about Yardley's makeup, which was quite interesting, and so I thought it wasn't so bad, it was quite nice, so after that I managed to go each month. In the September the Secretary of the Institute said her son in law had had a most terrible accident in Rugby and she was going to look after him, and out of the blue, goodness knows who thought of me, the President came round and asked me if I would take on as Secretary. I said I'd never done anything like that before in my life and I wouldn't know how to begin to write the minutes. She said I only needed to do it for three months and they'd have another vote, so I took it on for three months and did it for seven and a half years. I never did lose it.

Then I became President and I asked Mabel to be Secretary, and her response was the same as mine had been. She still did it though, same as me.

DAVID CLARABUT

Sailing, flying, war and peace.

David and Deirdre Clarabut outside The Old Rectory

18/11/98

We moved here to St. Mary's Hoo in September 1954. My wife found this house but it was in a hell of a mess, the fabric was OK but the garden was an absolute jungle and we could not walk on it. She told me she'd found the house we wanted so I went to see it. I got to the bottom of the drive and said, "I'm not buying a barn of a place like that" and went away. After a few months I came back and agreed to it. It had been empty since the end of the war. It has quite a history to it. When George IV was the Prince of Wales he had a mistress, Mrs. Fitzherbert, but he couldn't marry her because she was a Catholic, so he found a priest in Newgate Jail who would marry them if he got him out of jail, paid off his debts and gave him a parish way out in the country, so the Prince got him out of jail, paid off his debts and he gave him this parish. It was in his family for quite a long time. After the First War it was divided into flats and that's how it was until after the Second War. It had a retainer on it and was empty for quite a long time until I bought it.

It was very disappointing when the church was sold because it's a sort of sentiment really. When we came here we thought we could keep an average congregation of five. My wife is a Catholic and is in as much trouble as I am but we all went to church, the entire family, to keep the numbers up, but they eventually closed it down.

There have been remarkably little changes in the village really. We did have a chap who used to live in one of the cottages here who was on the city council who thought the village was a bit dead in the late fifties and thought he would try and liven it up a bit and get the council to develop it, but everybody got up in arms and he was very upset.

People wanted peace and quiet in the country. He was a nice chap and when he realised what the feeling was he backed down. It was only four years ago we got the preservation order.

I don't know who instigated it, but there is a representative of Rural England here. All development is banned in this preservation area. It is not a very big area. It includes the village and the church and church view as far down as where the Cleggs live. Most of the land round here is owned by the Church.

There had been a pub and a school, now closed, I don't know about a shop. There was a communal post box where the papers were delivered. I was told the pub was past the church and turn right and it was on that corner on the left hand side but it was a long time ago.

The villagers worship at St. Mary's and Allhallows now, and Stoke, which was a joint ministry. They have changed the ministries so that High Halstow, St. Mary Hoo and Allhallows come together, and Stoke does Stoke and Grain.

I was in the family shipping business in Rochester, which was started by my great grandfather and when he died at the end of the last century it was divided up into two, half to my grandfather and half to my great uncle. The brother was unsuccessful and went bust, but my grandfather was successful and flourished. We did a lot of trading in Malta, the Mediterranean, West Africa and round the coast of the UK and also New York and Bermuda. In 1965 that company, of which my uncle was chairman, was acquired by a city company, Hays Wharf, in those days. In 1968 I was invited to join the board of Hays Wharf and my last four years before I retired I ran the whole group.

The company down here was called London and Rochester Trading and there was Hays Wharf. My brother and I both joined Hays Wharf but he stayed down in Rochester and ran the business here. I went up to London to my office to become joint MD then MD then Chief Executive of the whole group.

I was a member of the Waterman's Company and was Master in 1972 and Shipwrights Company of which I was a Warden in 1982 so I got very much involved in that, leaving early in the morning and getting home late at night I didn't get involved with anything locally except with the RNLI. That's the only bit of local charity work I did.

I used to sail and Upnor was my main base. I had a series of five offshore boats, and I would sail the Medway and the Solent and competed, as did my brother and my grandfather. I had to give up racing and I tried to go cruising, but every time I saw a yacht on the horizon I had to chase it, so I gave it up altogether.

My grandfather had six children, three of whom died very early. My mother was the eldest, he had one surviving son who was Maurice Gill and he married Christine Brice and my Mother's surviving sister married Joe Brice from Mockbeggar who was Christine's brother, so a brother and sister married a sister and brother. Joe was my uncle by marriage.

War.

My first fright was a midair collision. That was when I was training in Canada. I had just got my wings and I was sent up and we were doing formation flying, very close together. He came up and went straight into my tail. You are taught to release your parachute just before you hit the water and I did. I landed on the ice on the lake and knocked myself out. The chap who hit me was still flying and he saw the hole in the ice, but couldn't see me. I could see land and struggled to it, and got to a house and finally got back to base. I was out of action for about a fortnight. That was just one little incident.

I did my initial training at an airbase in America just outside Detroit, then did my final training in Kingston, Ontario, and did my operational training in the UK. I knew a few pilots from the First War who flew in the Second War.

I went onto HMS Furious. The Courageous and the Glorious were sunk, and the other ship of the four was the Hermes. They put a flight deck on merchant ships. We were based off Norway, and my brother was in submarines. At one point we were dogging a German convoy and we were told that all submarines off Norway were hostile, but I knew my brother was nearby and I was very worried we might sink him by mistake.

I wanted to stay in after the war, but my eyes weren't good enough and they only wanted to keep the very best. I had transferred in 1943 and was a Royal Navy Reserve pilot.

I wasn't involved in bombing Germany itself, just at sea, protecting convoys and anti-submarine patrols and so on. When we were out to sea we were on permanent patrol. I was never shot down, but I was shot at by anti-aircraft fire. We had as many casualties outside operations as there were on operations.

A German battleship was tucked away under the mountains in Norway. The submarines had a go and the RAF couldn't get her because they bombed from high altitude, but we came in at a lower height, so we were sent in. She was surrounded by anti-aircraft guns and we had to fly through the barrage before we could drop our bombs. We had three carriers and six escort carriers. It was potentially quite dangerous for our ships to be out there and we had to get on and off as quickly as possible so we sent one of our squadrons to the Victorious and one of theirs to the Furious. We took off first and then the next wing took off an hour later. Eighteen planes took off initially, nine on each wing.

We did a lot of flying over an island on a loch in Scotland, approximately the same size as a German battleship and used as a target for practicing dive bombing. When the water was very flat you couldn't see where the surface of the water was and we lost a few aeroplanes like that.

Betty Wright – born Betty Blackman 28 January 1920

Teaching, toilets, wickedness and the Queen coming to visit on washday.

My grandmother was Emma Barty and she was born on the first of June 1859 at Sharnal Street. She married my grandfather Jon Blackman on 2 May 1882, they lived at the Chequers Hoo – my great uncle had the Chequers and the Bells and he put his brother into the Chequers. My grandmother didn't like bar work and she wasn't going to have it so they moved up to Pierces Farm in Hoo, which they rented. It's right opposite the bottom of Kingsnorth Terrace down to Bakers Terrace. It's the whole of the Knights Road, Miskin Road housing estate. He farmed that until 1911 when Kings Hill Farm came on the market.

Kings Hill Farm, according to the old deeds, was part of Ducks Court Farm – it doesn't seem possible with it being the other side of the road does it? But they bought Kings Hill Farm. My father had a job under the government and he gave up his job and worked with my grandfather on the farm and they kept cows. My father did a milk round in the village and my grandfather did a town milk round to places like Shorts, Ayling and Porters, the big factories – not to the actual houses.

Somehow or other my grandfather got into money difficulties. He was a man that would go to sales and buy lots of things unnecessarily and the land part of the mortgage was retrieved by my grandmother. But the buildings on the land had been paid for by my father, the cowshed, the stables and the house. They had been paid for directly to the builder by my father.

I remember my grandmother as a tall thin woman always dressed in black with a great big white apron. She was a very hard worker – a founder member of the Mothers Union and she used to make butter and sell it, having taken the cream of the milk. My grandfather taking the milk into town, was had up for his milk being deficient in fat several times. But she had made the butter – the butter and eggs were the farmer's wife's perks. She made the money and that was how she was able to redeem the mortgage.

After my grandfather died in 1927, she wanted my father out of the house. She said that it belonged to her, that the whole lot belonged to her, and there was a lot of trouble – the case actually went to the High Court. It wasn't settled until I was 15 – that would be 1935 – and the builder, a Mr. Cracknell who had emigrated to America or Canada somewhere, was actually fetched home to prove my father had paid for the buildings.

When the matter was settled we had to pay her a very small sum – the amount of half the actual land. The land involved being all that at the Fourwents where the BP club is built, where the army camp was. That was the land. As I say I haven't any fond memories of my grandmother at all. It was all just rows and rows.

She didn't want my father to marry at all, the others had all emigrated to Australia, Arthur and Len, dad wouldn't go with them. He said they couldn't all leave home, somebody must stay, and he had always worked under the government and taken his money home. Then he met my mother– he had apparently been engaged three times but eventually he met my mother and he wanted to get married. So as I say, the house was rebuilt and the cowshed was done.

The day he wanted to get married, he said to my grandfather, will you lend me 7 and sixpence, and my grandfather said whatever for and my father told him ' I'm getting married'. My grandfather said,' For Christsakes boy don't let your mother know!'

And she was so angry about it that she went up the garden path with a stick in one hand and a brick in the other and she was going to break every window in the house. So that's how my mother started off married life.

In November 1918 my mother was desperately ill and my father also had the flu at that time. Mother had pneumonia and pleurisy and a premature birth and lost my brother. I was told by a person who lived across the road and looked after mother, that my grandmother would ask how my father was but never once did she mention my mother– although three doctors said there was nothing they could do for her. It was the Airforce doctor who lived in Bells Lane, in the Terrace, who apparently saved her life – so the story goes.

My grandmother had no time for me at all, the only grandchild she had any time for was my sister Doris – one Christmas she bought Doris a present – a miller that went up and down a pole and bought down a sack of corn on his head and my mother took it back to her and said, 'You've got three grandchildren – if you can't give to all, don't give to any'.

I cannot ever remember her giving me anything, nothing at all. She used to make ice cream, which she sold at the house, and I can remember the little ha'penny and penny cornets.

Now, past the house, further out, on what is now the Kings Hill estate – there was a plot of land – fruit trees - the Far Plot we called it. If she was out in the Far Plot, my grandfather would call us, beckon to us, 'Come on. Come On' and he'd give us a little ha'penny cornet each. But we never got any if she was around. She wouldn't give you anything, nothing at all. My grandfather died of cancer when I was seven and there was a terrible row the last time he went to hospital and she told him never to come back again. Well he did, he came back and he died at home.

When I retired I was doing visiting for the blind and I met a woman whose mother had lived opposite to us and knew all about it. This woman, she was older than me, used to go for rides with my grandfather when he took the milk into town. And she told me that her mother looked after him when he was dying, not my grandmother.

My grandmother had a younger son, the youngest who she lost as a baby. She lost her first baby, Emma, then there was Martha, then my father, then Len, then the youngest one, James. My father was always blamed for his death. At the time he was born they were living in Pearce's farmhouse and my dad was an absolute daredevil. He was always into everything. I think that's why I always liked little boys who were naughty when I was at school! Always preferred the naughty ones – I could see my dad all over again, you know.

He was told not to go into the field near the horses and there was one particular horse he wanted to show off on. He wanted to show his friends he could ride on it bareback, which he did, but he was thrown. The boys ran up to the house shouting 'Mrs Blackman, your Willy's dead, your Willy's dead' She went running down to get him to find out what happened. It was the day she got up from having Jim, James, the youngest one, and she said that the shock caused her milk to curdle and that killed the baby. So my father always had the blame for the baby dying! (*Betty laughs*).

I can remember rows when I was a child with Mrs. Whitehead, who also lived on the estate. Especially when mushrooms were in the area. There was a time when they hit the Chatham News – they had smashed mushrooms in each others eyes and ruined their glasses (Betty *really* laughs). In between they were quite friendly but always at mushroom time this blew up – because they both would claim the mushrooms.

Kings Hill Estate in 1911/1913 – not too sure, was sold in plots for housing. Mr. Raymus, an auctioneer from Sheerness, came up to sell the plots and my grandfather went to pick him up from the station, Chatham or Rochester, not sure which and the plots were auctioned off. We owned some plots but not the whole lot. They belonged to so many people – mostly Londoners. The plot opposite where the cow shed was, that was a large plot, that was down as the plot for a hotel and I have a deed somewhere that says no building of value less than £200 must be built on the land – the King's Hill estate. Nothing less than £200.

I don't know who owned them originally, but a lot of Londoners owned them. My mother used to send them butter every year – a peppercorn rent but butter. That's why the estate was never fenced in because although we had grazing rights for the peppercorn rent you had to be out with the cows all the time. You had to mind the cows. That was one of my chores as a child. It was such a lonely job – stuck out on that estate watching they didn't get at peoples' gardens and that sort of thing. Anyway both my grandmother and Mrs Wright both thought they owned the mushroom rights so that's how that all blew up.

I've always been led to believe my grandmother had a pension from the Australian government for Len. He was killed at Villers Bretagne and when she was old enough for the old age pension, she had too much money. She couldn't get the old age pension. Len left some money – not a lot, £700 and something that was shared – she had half of it, Dad had a quarter and his sister Martha had a quarter. It was with Martha's money that she came home from Australia – I don't think she could have afforded to come home if her brother hadn't died.

They came home from Australia and lived with the old lady at first, until she fell out with them. Then they moved into a big barn at Parbrook – the Beaumonts lived in that area. It might have belonged to the Miskins, I don't know. So she'd rowed with them and they left. Anyway, when she (the grandmother) was old enough for the old age pension and couldn't get it, she gave Martha a thousand pounds, which in those days was a lot of money. She had owned Donkey field and Donkey Meadow at the back there, that was part of Sharnal Street. Well, Martha had the house built that is now Thorne's Nursery, and that cost £1000 to build. It was built by Pattenden at Rochester. That was about 1930.

I remember my cousin Grace when she was going with one boy, going up there, that must have been 1935, 36 – I remember because Martha was left handed and I was so glad my mother wasn't because when Martha walloped Jack or Grace it was the wedding ring that caught them!

Anyway Martha had the house built and it was very elaborate stuff inside on the walls – something like what they do on the ceilings now but it was on all the walls on all the house (Artex?) but it was supposed never to want decorating but Thornes, I know, have done something with it – they couldn't live with it any longer.

Martha moved there from the Homestead which was a little bungalow which was bordering what it know Kings Hill Drive – where it comes out by the shops on Bell Lane, up the top, where the stackyard was. As you go along there was a bungalow, at the very end, called the Homestead where in the 14-18 war a German woman, Ketchy Mupil lived but apparently the village boys led her a hell of a life. Then there was Mrs. Whiteheads house as you came through the estate. I remember Chris (Rigby) coming there once and the place was a bit untidy and Grace said put this away, put this away and I shoved the butter under a cushion on the armchair and he sat on it. (more laughter)

So she moved from there to Emohruo, which is Our Home, backwards. She wasn't there very long before her mother was sending her solicitor's letters; she'd got the state pension and now she wanted her thousand pounds back. So Martha had to sell the house and give her the money back. Money was my grandmother's God, it really was.

She used to grow beautiful flowers, she had a lovely garden, and during the war soldiers would go there for bouquets of flowers to take home to their wives. Well normally a bunch of flowers was sixpence or a shilling in those days. But she would cut them a lovely bouquet and she'd say, 'There, aren't they beautiful, won't your wife be pleased when you take her these', and they'd say 'yes, how much are they?' and she'd say ' well, I'm only a poor old widow woman, you give me what you think.' And usually they'd give her about half a crown.

She honestly, this is the honest truth, she died clutching her handbag. That is the honest truth. It contained £700, she was going to take it with her. She'd put all her things ready for her funeral but unfortunately we didn't find them until after she was buried (*peals of laughter*) All her best nightie and all that sort of thing but she went off in her second best. I think she was 96 when she died, she was well into her nineties anyway. She fell and broke her hip when she was 91 – at Christmas, in the snow, we had snow that year. And in the spring she was out in the Far Plot planting potatoes – that was her determination, you know.

My sister Doris, Mrs. Brookes, is just the same, determination. You can't say don't do it to her at all. I don't know. I suppose, in a way, you have to admire it don't you. But I've always been the type, 'why do today what you can put off 'til tomorrow!'

Towards the end, when she was ill, my mother didn't actually look after her, my father looked after her, but my mother had made her beef tea and egg custards and all that you feed people like that with you know. How my mother did that for her I don't know because, I couldn't, the life she led us, I couldn't have done anything for her.

None of us went to her funeral, well my father did and her nephew Jimmy Chesterton and his wife. On the day of the funeral I was putting my niece and nephew on the bus to go home from school and a member of the Mothers Union came along and said, 'I've just been to your grandmother's funeral, you weren't there'

And I said, 'No, I wasn't I only had one grandmother, my grandmother Cruttenden and I went to her funeral seven years ago'.

I did say to my Dad before the funeral that if he wanted me to go to support him I would. He said, 'I wouldn't ask you to, I know the life she led you'.

When I was 8, I was dressed up in a little pink dress and I was taken to court and she was bound over to leave me alone. (Betty is quiet for a minute, sadness gets the better of her and the interview it stopped until she recovers.)

Thank you. As I said before, I am Betty Blackman and I have two sisters, Doris and Peggy. Also, my mother was the eldest of seven and she had a sister who married an airman from King's North aerodrome and she married him when I was 10 days old and went abroad to Egypt for 2 ½ years, when he came home, he got married quarters in

Suffolk – Martlesham? And they went away. But she was the one daughter who had always stayed at home and served in the shop – my grandmother (Crittenden) had a sweet shop in the village, next to the post office. And she wouldn't stay there, she was so homesick, he got fed up with her and brought her back again. And so my sister Doris being a fairly new baby, they let her take me, to keep me there, and so I spent a lot of time with my aunt and uncle until my cousin Bobby was born and I was 6. I think that was one of the things that my grandmother Blackman had against me, that I was so much in the other side's family.

I do remember being at Martleshem and I got a good smack one day because Queen Alexandra came to visit. She used to come and visit the camp on a Monday Morning and my aunt was doing the washing and she locked the door. We were in Sergeant Majors' Quarters, right at gate and this day, she came to us at the gate and my Aunt told me to be quiet and pretend she was out and I made a noise and she had to let Queen Alexandra in and I got a good smack for it.

I lived with them until I was six, when Bobby was born, but Bobby and I were always very, very close. I was never jealous of him. I think I was closer to him actually than a sister. When he came home from Africa he came here, he didn't go to his mother who at that time was living in Cambridgeshire. He came to me. He used to bring his girlfriends here – Gum Noster (?), Beryl Stopps – they were two – they didn't come here, they used to wait for them across the road – for Norman and Bobby. And Norman and Bobby would be in the other room laughing at them with the rain pouring down as they stood under the awning.

I didn't pass the 11+ - very few people did in those days. My mother was desperate for me to teach, I think she always wanted to teach, so she paid for me to go to the grammar school. I went there, things got difficult with my grandmother money wise and we had to pay her some money, and the headmistress didn't want me to leave and I had a free place for my last 2 years at the grammar school.

From the Grammar school, I wanted to go to college to teach and I knew that I needed a Kent training scholarship. In a Kent training scholarship they gave you so much money and lent you so much – they wouldn't give you any without lending some – it meant that you had to come back in Kent to teach for three years, paying back a pound a month in the first year, £2, in the second – then £3 a month, so I applied for a job as an unqualified teacher to prove that I could teach to get this scholarship and I got a letter on a Saturday morning to attend at Charlton Hatch on the Monday morning. Now nobody had ever heard of Charlton Hatch – where on earth was it? Uncle George Cruttenden, he had a three wheeler car, BSA, you know, and he took me down with a case on the Monday morning – I was 18.

I'd got to find digs and live there if I could. I went into school, the caretaker was there and she took me in and I boarded there for 15 shillings a week Monday to Friday, 18 shillings if I stayed weekends. I stayed there 2 years and I got the training scholarship.

I went for the interview and the inspector said 'Have you had any inspectors in', and I said 'yes', and he asked 'who?' So I said, 'Mr Vickers', he said 'you're quite sure it was Mr .Vickers' I said 'yes'. He said 'well I'm Mr Vickers' and it wasn't him it was someone else!

From there I went to Stockport College where I got married. When I left I applied to Higham – there were two jobs going, one at Higham and one at Hoo. Well I didn't want to come home (Hoo) because I thought everybody knew me, so I applied to Higham – I had a very nice letter back from a Mr. Hutchinson who said he was very sorry but he couldn't employ me because I was a married woman and it was a permanent post and married women were not allowed to hold permanent posts in those days.

So I wrote to Kent and said, 'Right, if you want your money back you've got to give me a job.' By that time, the job was still going at Hoo and the headmistress and chairman of the governors, Sir Edmund Waters, had been on to my father to persuade me to come to Hoo. So I came back to Hoo for 24 years. An inspector came in and I did some lecturing for her at Kingsgate College and she kept on at me about moving. Mrs. Dann didn't want me to go but I realised she was going to retire and I felt it wouldn't have been fair for a new Head if I was still there. I was infant trained so I always had so much of my own way – Dorothy Dann was secondary trained. She was a history specialist. She only came home because her mother had died and she came home to look after her brother.

I wouldn't have worked easily under a younger person, I'm sure, having had my own way for so long. Dorothy used to go home to Linton and ask him, if I'd suggested something, ask Linton what he thought of it. Now what did

Linton know about teaching? Then she'd come back and say, well Linton thinks it will be alright and we'd do whatever.

Well, I applied and got the Headship at St.Michaels in Maidstone, which was really lovely, I loved it there. It sounds snobbish but there wasn't a council house in my catchment area – everybody was working and earning and buying their own house – do you know what I mean? A different atmosphere, and again a Church school. It was a completely different atmosphere. An inspector came in one day and said 'How much longer do you intend to sit here' and I said ' what do you mean?' and he said ' well there are two new ones coming up nearer home for you and you'd be a fool not to apply for them. I want you to apply for both of them and I'll back you all the way.'

I was so happy at St. Michaels I didn't want to move – it was when they were doing the Bluebell hill round. Well I went to Dean's wood and that was exactly the same distance as St. Michaels so I wasn't really interested but I did apply. And I applied for the Bly and I got the Bly. Now that was wonderful because it was a brand new school.

One of the women I used to work with at Hoo, she said go and get a Headship and I'll come as your deputy so I asked her. She said I can't I can't – so I asked her husband to work on her. A new school like that, you've got to equip it and everything, I knew together we could make a good job of it. She came as deputy and my deputy at ST. Michaels, which wasn't such a big school, came as senior mistress, grade 3. So at the top of the school we had 3 people all working on the same lines and I think we made a very good job of the Bly. I had 11 years there before I retired. Unfortunately both those teachers are dead now.

I enjoyed every minute of my teaching life, I wouldn't have done anything else.

My family all laugh and say it was all about toilets – I can't remember the toilets at Charlton Hatch but then I had trouble with the boys' toilets at St. Michaels because they were all open and the rain came in. There was trouble with the toilets at Hoo because old man Franks only came to empty the buckets (there were no flushing toilets until the 1950's in Hoo – only dry closets that were emptied daily) on a Monday morning when the dinner was being delivered. I got the boys' toilets roofed at St. Michaels and they made the roof so it sloped and it sloped so all the water went down into the girls' toilets, so instead of the boys getting wet the girls did. Anyway we got that sorted out. Then I had trouble with the toilets at the Bly because every toilet had been set on porous cement and every time I reported that the toilets were leaking, the office said it was the children misbehaving. It wasn't, every toilet in that school, 26 toilets, every one had to be taken out and replaced and they smashed every toilet – they couldn't put them back again.

There was a Dr. Swain lived at The Elms – that's a coincidence as there is a doctor there now, his wife went to the chapel and it got to the knowledge of the Rev, Benson and when she went to the church on Sunday morning he refused her Holy Communion because she'd been seen to enter the dissenters chapel. This went on for some time, many letters were exchanged until the High Canterbury Court ordered the reverend to give her Holy Communion. Apparently he wouldn't, he never did.

He was the vicar who melted down the communion set and half the silver was made into a smaller one and nobody knew what happened to the rest.

Do you know the workhouse, where Dr. Wall lived? I can remember the men being marched down to the church. They weren't allowed to sit in the body of the church, they had to sit up in the North Aisle, which is now the Church room. I remember going to the sale with my father, my father bought a smokers bow chair you know, and I remember how cold the concrete was, it struck up through your feet you know. The men were this end and the women's block was the other end and the last baby born in there was about the same age as my sister Peg.

Do you remember Tom Broad the butcher? It was his nephew. One of his sisters married Mr Cairns, another Mr. Snowdon and another Mr. Rands and Old Rands was randy and he left her on one occasion, and much to the family's disgust, she threw herself on the parish. Then the police would find him and bring him back – otherwise they wouldn't be doing with it.

So the son was born in the workhouse.

JAMES CASTLE (Farmer and Landowner)

Donated article from 1994

James Castle (right)

James Castle, Dagnam Farm, Allhallows is the son of the George Stewart Castle and Ivy Mary Amelia Muggeridge.

Jimmy Castle took the Cock pub at Grain around the beginning of the 19th century. He took a small piece of land at Frindsbury. His son, William Castle was born in 1829 and died in 1889. He expanded the land to 400 acres. He weighed 20 stone and had a pony to bring him from Frindsbury to North Street Farm and a different one to take him back. He had ploughing engines. He once drove an old pony across a steam engine cable when he was in a bad mood. William married a girl from Poole. He had a barge on the river and was a keen sailor as well as a farmer. He eventually sold the barge to the Vidgeon family. His son George was born in 1863 and died around 1928. He was also a big fellow and a member of the Stationers Livery Company. His brother William James Thomas was at Sharnal Street, then emigrated to Australia. The Batchelor family then took over at Sharnal Street. One of his sons died in the World War (his name is on a plaque in High Halstow church).

Around 1850, the Castles first moved from Grain to Frindsbury then to North Street at the end of the last century. Billy lived at North Street as did his son, George, who was born in 1863. Then to Bay Tree Farm around 1898 when James's father, George was born. He was the son of George Castle of Bay Tree farm and George's brother was "Ned". They both went into the 1914/18 War in the Army and returned to the farm. In the 1920's the post-war farming depression came in and the farm went into decline. The Church Commissioners owned the farm. James' father, George broke away and married Ivy Mary Amelia Muggeridge and went to Stone House Farm. "Ned" stayed on with his grandfather, William Castle, and carried on for a couple of years after his grandfather's death around 1928 and then sold up for financial pressures. "Ned" then set up a lorry business 'E. A. Castle' in Reed Court in Strood. This took farm produce to the markets in London. This was carried on by Gerald, a cousin of James.

George Castle went to Hoo Village School and was taught by David Dann's grandfather. He then joined the Army and drove lorries, taking shells to the front line at night. He was a non-commissioned rank. Latterly, he volunteered to join the Royal Flying Corps and was being trained as a navigator when the war finished.

The Muggeridge family were a very well-known family earlier this century. Richard Muggeridge was a salt shepherd, living in Stoke. He had no children by his first wife (nee Rayner) who died aged 46. His second wife Mary Bridger gave him several children, James born in 1861 (James' grandfather), Richard, John Moses and Amy. Amy married George Harbour (who was the wheelwright/carpenter in Middle Stoke). Amy was the headmistress of Stoke School.

Around 1860, Richard bought his first piece of land at Ward End, Stoke, consisting of 30 acres of land at a cost of £30 per acre. Richard was 52 years old when James was born and 69 when his last daughter Amy was born. He died in 1883.

James started up a coal business collecting coal from the station to the village. He married a Plewis and took some land at Grain, then moved to Binney Farm, where Ivy Muggeridge was born. The family then moved to Turkey Hall Farm. Around the turn of the century, Squire Dupper from Hollingbourne, owned Turkey Hall Farm, which at that time was derelict. James agreed with Squire Dupper that if he could rent the farm for two years free of charge, then he would pay a rent after the two years had expired. Two or three years later, James saw Squire Dupper again and agreed to have the same arrangement with Malmaynes Hall Farm. He took Binney because of shooting. He lived at Malmaynes then MacKay's Court.

Richard was the second brother. He started at Grain and had two sons, Arthur and Percy. He put Arthur in Dagnam when he got married. Around 1924/26, he bought Coombe Farm.

John went to Malmaynes, then went out to fight in Gallipolis. He got badly shellshocked, which affected him for the rest of his life. Malmaynes and Hoppers were then put on the market. Moses had Nord and Burneys Farms. He had a son called Moses, who had no children. At this stage, the three brothers owned nearly all the farm land on the Hoo Peninsula (except the land run by the Bett family). One by one the farms changed hands.

James Castle is the only surviving member of the Muggeridge and Castle families still farming on the Hoo Peninsula.

The area has really changed since James started farming. Early crops were at their peak at the beginning of the century. The potatoes and straw were taken by barge and horse manure was brought back. There were two wharves at MacKay's Court. Changes took place when the railway started up, going through Stoke to Allhallows and Grain. Corn and early vegetables used to be taken to London in bushel baskets, pex then half bushel bags. Greens and early potatoes were sold by Arthur Muggeridge who had a stand in London called J B Thomas.

Joe Jackson and James Castle, Ploughing match

Arthur went to the Derby and farmed Malmaynes. Around 1987, the supermarkets started buying early vegetables from abroad, which travelled in refrigerated transport. The crops in England were too unreliable.

James' grandfather, George, grew peas and early potatoes and he had casual labour from the village. James' father George had a tractor and trailer and would pick up a gang. At one time, double decker buses ferried casual labourers around

There are now 7 1/2 full time farm workers (including a Farm Manager) on James's land which is 1700 acres but 2000 including Frindsbury. Earlier this century, there would have been 7/8 full time farm workers on each farm. Some of the farm labourers' cottages have now been sold although just over half are still inhabitant by farm workers.

There was a close association between Charlie Tuff, MP and James's grandfather, George Castle. Charlie Tuff owned MacKay's until the turn of the century, when the marshes flooded. MacKay's was then taken over by James' grandfather. Bertram Tuff was killed in 1918 in the War.

Molly Bett

Bossy big sisters, servants and the Old Tin Lizzies.

I was born in 1914, I lived in the district all my live. I lived just up the road at a farm called Beluncle.

My father came down in 1910. A lot of farmers came down this way. He came down to Southend as a sort of trainee and then they bought Beluncle off the Miskin's. There was an old farmhouse in the yard there and it burnt down and they built Beluncle. They can't have built it very long , 1 or 2 years, and they moved to Whitehall and daddy bought Beluncle. That must have been before 1910. There is a stone beside Beluncle, Sidney Miskin laid the stone, the son, it's got the date on it.

My mother and father married in 1910, the year they took Beluncle. My mother came from a family of 19 children – all but two survived. The Harrison family. I only had two sisters and a brother but the generation before thought nothing of having 10 children.

Molly, Betty, Peggy and Jim

Daddy never talked about the farm in the house. We enjoyed the countryside life but we weren't really interested in the farming. We didn't know the price of apples or anything like that. We had a dozen horses or more and about 27 men. It's different now, 3 tractors and three men to do the same work. It all happened slowly. We kept a horse for a long time at Beluncle because you couldn't get a tractor through the orchards. Jim had a horse right up until the time he died. He wouldn't have parted with it for anything.

I went to Gad's Hill School. I was a weekly boarder, prep school in Rochester first. Jim went to Miss Snowdon. There were only about 30 pupils at Gad's Hill when I was there. The headmistress was Miss. Burke. She was about so tall with a filthy temper. There were 2 or 3 classes – and of course the army had it during the war. They improved the cloakrooms.

I was married by the first years of the war. After school I trained as a nursery nurse in London. But then things change so much don't they? My parents wouldn't let me have a job as a nanny, they thought it was awful I'd trained as a nurse, so I came home and acted as chauffeur to my mother who couldn't drive. It wasn't the right thing to do to go out and work. The war changed everything. Women didn't reckon to go and work before that.

They hadn't minded me being away so much when my sister was home but then she got married and I became the family chauffeur.

Peggy Crawford is my older sister, then there was me, then my brother, James Meakle who died quite a while ago and then my younger sister, she was christened Muriel Wallace and she's always been called Bun. I don't think she'd answer to Muriel. The Scottish name for baby is Bunty and then the youngest member of the family was always called baby until the next one came along. So she was called Bunty. It was shortened to Bun and has been Bun all her life.

I think things changed during the war. The men weren't there so the women went out to work. I didn't work because I was on the farm but other women did and they got used to earning money. We used to have children from the school , about 14 who would come as housemaids and cooks and if one left they would be queuing up for the job – for 10 bob a week.

Kathy asks – 'what's that?'

Oh, aren't you awful! About 50p. I was talking to one of the kids last week and they didn't know what sixpence was. Yes 50p a week and you fed them and looked after them. Some were good, some weren't so bad.

A cuckoo clock interrupts.

We used to play in the watercourse – catching tiddlers. We used to go down to the sea wall. We could go swimming down on the Saltings. We used to clear a path on one particular strip down to the bay to go swimming. We had an Uncle John (McLennan Robertson) when we were small, he used to go down with us. He was a wonderful character. He was invalided out of the army in the first war and came down to live on the farm. He was meant to be looking after the chicken or something but he never did a stroke of work. We used to go picking blackberries with Doug's grandfather, at Fenn Street. We'd have big baskets and Uncle Jock would be sitting waiting with a big basket full of blackberries and then when we got home we'd find he'd filled it up with grass and just put the blackberries on the top.

He had a bicycle before we were big enough to cycle ourselves and my sister used to sit on the step at the back and I would sit on the cross bar and he'd take us all down the marshes to go swimming. When we were bigger we'd go on our own bikes. He taught me my alphabet, how to tell the time – he was wonderful. He lived in one of the farm cottages.

He kept a greyhound and a lurcher and we'd go hare-coursing across the farm. The dogs would never kill them though and I never could kill them.

My mother died quite early and then I more-or-less took over the house until I was married. I had a cottage too, a tumble down cottage on the farm and I'd do the garden. A little cottage in the stackyard – The Crumbles. It was empty for a long, long time when I was about 20. I kept saying I wanted to do the garden. We had a boy who did the Beluncle garden but he didn't do anything down there.

I remember one day and we'd been wanting rain for ages and it rained. I said to my father again could I have the garden and he was so delighted with the rain he said yes, I could have the key in the morning – so I took over.

I grew flowers – no particular favourites. I cleared the rubbish away and found what had been there before. I used to take the children there for a picnic later. I think they've knocked it down now. It was a large garden and a tiny cottage – 2 rooms and a sort of scullery with a copper in it. It would have been an old couple living in it. They would have lived in it for years. They would have grown vegetables. It's like Cecil up here – he doesn't know which way to turn there is so much work and only two of them. Though I must admit he keeps me in vegetables. Why he grows so much I don't know. Habit I suppose.

We used to provide all our own vegetables from the kitchen garden. The rest of the groceries would be delivered by Mr. Dann. You'd order one day and he'd deliver it the next. Then there was Stopps the butcher and Webbs opposite him. If you wanted fish it came out on the bus – we'd go up to Hoo and collect it from the bus depot. A depot where the parcels would be left from Rochester. The fish came from Jenkins and he'd put it on the bus in Rochester.

Doug: Before the bus there were carriers – the Shearmans , my uncle was a carrier for a while, one of the Mortley's was a carrier. They'd have a horse and van and they would collect orders one day then go into Rochester, get the parcels and come home and deliver it.

Molly: I used to go to Hoo Church – 'til the vicar got a bit High Church, daddy being Scottish was very Low Church – Presbyterian – that was the end of the family going. My sister and I still used to go.

I was only saying the other day – the Miskins had a pony and trap and we used to go to church in that. We'd get a lift home – we'd walk there. You thought nothing of walking to Hoo. People would think you were mad now wouldn't they?

Doug: Yes – my mother used to walk to Rochester!

Molly: Well Jims favourite occupation was to follow the cattle into (Rochester) market with the drover. He thought nothing of walking from Beluncle to Rochester market.

We were talking about bus fares – Ian (Bett) said it's about £5.00 return to the town hall from Stoke. I said we used to stop the bus at the gate of Beluncle and a return to the town hall was a shilling – 5p!

Sands had a private bus from Hoo, he had a little paper shop in Hoo.

There wasn't much for children to do. I think adults had a much more social life in those days – bridge parties and things like that – tennis parties up at High Halstow, Longfield was always having parties. I used to play – I was quite good at school but I had a rather domineering sister and she always reckoned she was much better than I was. I used to say well go off and play by yourself then! The funny thing was we didn't get on as children and we don't get on especially well now. It was always the same batch of people who played tennis. Everywhere had tennis courts in those days.

We used to play cricket on a Sunday evening on the lawn. We weren't supposed to. It wasn't the done thing to play cricket on a Sunday, so every time it was about time for the bus to be due my father would say we'd have to abandon the game until the bus went by so we weren't caught out playing cricket on a Sunday! We should have gone to church 2 or 3 times but no cricket or anything like that.

Doug: When I was first confirmed I'd go to communion, then 11 o clock service then Evensong – that was at High Halstow.

Molly: That was a nice church – we used to go there with Mr Harrison and my Aunt Wynnie. We always used to do the decorating at Easter time. We always went primrosing up at the woods in Chattenden on Good Friday so we didn't have to eat cod. I didn't like it – we used to have to have it for lunch on Good Friday. We used to take the primroses up to the church on the Saturday and do the windowsills –

lovely. I knew Halstow church better than I knew Hoo really. I'd go to Hoo Church for the services but at High Halstow it was quite fun.

Doug: I was christened at High Halstow. Christened and confirmed.

Molly: I was christened at Hoo but I wasn't much part of the Church Community there. My sister used to play the organ. Same sister (*laughs heartily!*) She learnt to play the organ and would go to Hoo to practise – in those days you'd need someone to pump it. She'd get me to do that. One thing I would do, to relieve the boredom was to see how near I could get to letting it run out (*peel's of giggles*) before I pumped it again. A little weight would come down and you'd let it come down as far as it would before it run out!

Once Jim (Molly's brother) came with us and got up in the pulpit – he was letting forth in the pulpit – Peggy was on the organ and we suddenly turned round and the vicar was standing in the back of the church!

We had a series of doctors – I wrote a list out for Dr. Rigby going back to Trubridge who was supposed to be a spy in the First World War. He was supposed to be a German spy or so we were told. The airships were on the marshes – we had two big airships down there and a whole lot of the army at what they call Berry Wiggins now. The army quarters. The hangers were there for ages up to about 20 or 30 years ago. I don't know what happened to Trubridge. Dr.Coombe came next.

I remember Dr. Wall – he was an extremely clever Doctor.

Doug: He was my godfather and I loved him very much

Molly: Was he really? A very nice man with a very bad temper. It used to terrify me to ring him up. I'd be so glad if I got Mabel instead of him. I think his wife's name was Betty. Dr. Wall used to drink whisky galore but he always used to like milk in it. Always used to stop at Court Lodge for whisky and milk. On the other hand if you wanted him as a doctor he was extremely clever.

Doug: I told Kathy how if he was called out of the district late at night and if he wanted a whisky on the way home, he would call in at your house and help himself.

Molly: Whisky and Milk. He was a good chap – they lived in the Red House below the Spire down in Hoo. Same side of the road as the supermarket. The he went to live where the workhouse was – next to the Elms – a long low, dark place. People didn't like him, who used to be on his panel, because he used to prescribe things they could buy at the chemist like aspirin and so on – probably very rightly – rather than go to town.

We always reckoned it was because of Dr, Wall that Ian is still alive – they thought he had Pyloric Stenosis when he was six weeks old and operated at Great Ormond Street, but he didn't. I had to you see – it was twins – they didn't know it was going to be twins until they arrived. Gill was Ian's twin.

Ian was poorly right from the beginning. He started with a broken arm – they had to take him to St. Bart's to have his arm set. He's got one arm ½ inch shorter than the other one.

They were delivered at home – the doctor delivered them eventually, they were the wrong way round and two of them – but that's beside the point. He was very poorly and kept spewing up all this black stuff and they thought it was Pyloric Stenosis and took him to Great Ormond's Street and operated and then decided it wasn't and he just got worse and worse.

In those days we had Dr. Blair from Strood – why do doctors all drink? We'll pass over that shall we? Anyway we got so worried about Ian that Phillip stopped the old Dr. Wall in the village one day and asked him to come and see Ian because we were so worried about him.

He came to see him and said, because they always said it was blood he was spitting up, and he said it's not blood it's bile. He gave us some little tablets called Dover tablets – that you're not allowed to have anymore – tiny grey tablets and they cured him, just like that. The operation didn't help but these little tablets cured him. They were some sort of dope because you could give them to children who were teething and were terribly upset and it would calm them down. They made them illegal after a while.

Nurse Carr was the district nurse and midwife before Nurse Leaman (cuckoo clock chimes again). Nurse Carr got about by bicycle. We all contributed to buy Nurse Leaman her first car. Nurse Leaman had a nursing home at Stoke – this was before the NHS.

Nurse Leahman and her Mother.

Doug: Nurse Leaman came in about 1928 because she always used to say she borned my sister but she never borned me!

Molly: I met my husband when he was 11 and I was 11. I met him at the point to point. He came from Liverpool – he used to come and stay with Uncle Bert who lived at Court Lodge and I suppose we were kids and much the same age we used to all meet up. We used to go to the Point to Point at Sutton Valance. We always reckoned that's when we got together.

I didn't see him much after that until Uncle Bert got ill and he came to help with the farm. He was there, well he took over in the end.

Robert Bett, Uncle Bert, came from a farm in Lincolnshire – there were 4 boys and the doctor said that old Mrs Bett – Uncle's mother, if they didn't get her out of Lincolnshire she would die. So they decided to move to Kent. She actually lived to be 90.

Robert Bett

Anyway they came down and looked at the farm and took over the Court Lodge lease. It belonged to the commissioners by that time. So they set out from Lincolnshire with all the tackle, all the horse, all the wagons, all the men – lock, stock and barrel – the whole lot. It took them 2 days – I'm not sure where they spent the first night but the second night was in Dartford. Then they got to Court Lodge the next day. Uncle Bert rode ahead to book the rooms where they would stay – it was a whole circus, all the wagons, all of them came, families and everyone, Lincolnshire to Stoke.

In those days there used to be a little train that came down – if you gave the driver a shilling, 5p, he would stop at the Halt for you, on the farm. There was a little station down there – not manned or anything. It was used for all the goods going to London. There used to be railway cottages down there – and there was a station at Beluncle – all our stuff would have gone to London by rail to the wholesale market.

Then there was a lorry that came to the farm. The Vidgeons had a lorry that carted produce – and the Rainer's carted produce.

Doug: We were very much independent in those days – I used to look over the fence, still do , to see what David Bucknall and Phillip Bett are doing – or Phillip would see what I was doing and go and tell Mrs. Bett. Give her a laugh!

Molly: I can't think what Doug's out in that cabbage field for!

Doug: We had a great time. I miss Phillip very much – we used to have great conversations. Arguments. We'd argue about anything under the sun!

Molly: Trouble was he'd come home and continue the argument. I, invariably without thinking would take the opposite side. It used to lead to great trouble, you and your arguments.

Doug: Yes I know. I'm sorry about that – it just happened.

Molly: Phillip used to argue for the sake of arguing. If you said something he would argue with it. Trouble was, being fairly reasonable I'd say the same as Doug. We'd fall out quite often!

Doug: He used to get really quite annoyed but the next day, we'd have a gin, and it would all be forgotten about.

Molly: I used to help with pay packets and things – I have run the farm when Phillip was laid up – with the help of the men I kept it going – but I mostly did secretarial work that sort of thing.

Doug: Yes Phillip didn't have very good health did he?

Molly: No He was ill on and off, and when he wasn't ill he thought he was. He wore out several of the doctors! Shame.

The war made a tremendous difference to how we lived – instead of having 2 or 3 servants in the house one buckled to and did it your elf. We never went back to that because the servant people, well they got far better jobs. The value of money changed - dramatically.

Doug: Yes – no-one had a car before the war. My father had one just before the war but it was only really the doctors and maybe a family like yours would have had one.

Molly: We had the first Buick that was made in Kent. The engine came from America and Shorts on the Esplanade did the bodywork – it was a wonderful open tourer – bright yellow. It had a sort of hood that you let down obviously and then it had a windscreen round for the back passengers as well that you could put up, it was a wonderful car.

We used to go to Scotland – my father came from Scotland so we used to go up there. He liked touring but the first day we had to be up at the crack of dawn because he reckoned we had to be 100 miles away before we had breakfast. We always made it but 100 miles now isn't as far as it was in those days.

Doug: That's quite an achievement if you remember what the roads were like. It wasn't the traffic

Molly: No – we only saw bicycles, everybody would go to work by bicycle and we used to swear at them. Do you remember Tin Lizzies? The old Fords? We had one of the first Tin Lizzies (Model T Ford) and that's what I went to school in. My father had one of the first cars down here that was a Belsize. 2 seater with a dickie – sort of like the boot – the boot came up and you'd sit in there. I think that was toward the end of the war. Maybe just after the war.

In Scotland they had one of the first cars there ever was in those days you had to put it in reverse to go up a hill because it went better in reverse.

Kathy: Apart from your family who else were seen as 'pillars of the community?'

Molly: I suppose the Brices were ones you always looked up to. Whether for the right reasons I don't know.

They would have been living at Hoo Lodge. I always thought of the Brices as being slightly superior.

Kathy: There is still a lot of respect for the boss at Mockbeggar (*Brice owned*) – they call Nick (*my husband and then farm manager at Mockbeggar*) Mr. Nick and me Mrs. Nick!

Doug: Do they really? My chaps at Cliffe – the ones I kept after I left Gattons, they always called me Mr. Marsh, there was never any Doug or anything like that. My lot at Brick House used to call me everything under the sun!

Molly: Don't you think it was probably because you worked with them when you were young?

Doug: Probably yes. I grew up with them.

Molly: That's the same with Ian (Bett) he grew up with them and you can't suddenly turn around and start calling them Mr. Bett. Most round here have grown up on the farm. One of the chaps working on the farm, he and Nigel spent their lives playing together. He can't call him Mr. Bett.

Doug: Do you remember Henry Pye?

Molly: Indeed I do. He was a great fellow he lived with Emmeline, his very strange sister. They originally came from St. Mary's Hall and farmed Court Lodge before Uncle took it.

Ian, Phillip and Phillipa Bett

He was extraordinary person – eccentric.

They lived where Andrew Brice lives now – after Henry Pye gave up farming. They were quite well off but behaved as if they didn't have a penny. They built the conservatory on the back of Broadwood and I went up and had to officially open the conservatory for them – I was about so big (Molly indicates a small child's height).

He used to ride around on a bicycle – going back to the bridge parties. Everyone in winter used to have a bridge party – everyone went to everyone else's sort of thing. One of the highlights was going up to Broadwood to the Pye's – it was always perishing cold. Henry lived in his overcoat – they never had a fire or anything like that. There was a marvellous statue at the bottom of the stairs and the guests, Brice was the worst, would drape this statue with hats and coats.

The thing about these bridge parties was everyone would try and out do everyone else as to what they supplied for eats. Emmeline always used to supply cold rice pudding. I used to take Emmeline out in the car quite often when I got back to my driving at Beluncle. I used to take her out – she never went out anywhere. I think Henry must have died by then. I can't remember.

Before that you'd always see him up the village on his bicycle. He had another sister – Mrs Hitchcock. She first married a Miskin and when he died she married Dr.

Hitchcock. Then there was Marian at Sharnal Street. She was fun. There were 3 sisters and Henry.

It was Henry who laid the whole of Court Lodge with Shell Drains. Drained the district. In those days they didn't have drains so they'd make a trench and fill the whole thing up with cockle shells and that would drain it.

Doug: My mother and her sister lived at Clinch Street, with my grandfather – he was the foreman for Henry Pye and he laid a shell path from Clinch Street to St. Mary's school so they could walk to school on a shell path.

Molly: Tell me, talking about Clinch Street, was there an oast house there.

Doug: Not to my knowledge – there was a granary that you used to go up steps to.

Molly: Mr Wilmot came down and called in to see me and he'd got a picture that was supposed to be Clinch Street

Doug: When I thought of Clinch Street I thought of where Arthur lives now – further down on the left hand side, where David his son lives, there's another little farm – I think it's Stout Farm – there's an oast house there. So not at Clinch Street no.

Molly: Mr. Wilmot wanted to find out where it was –
he did your barn didn't he – Hilda painted your barn at St.
Mary's' and this was another Hilda and he'd been told it was
Clinch Street.

Doug: Roland Hilda did a lot of sketches up there –
but when they became a picture they became a picture out of
his mind – you know!

Molly: I used to go up there with Arthur's grandfather,
he'd take us up to see the herons and go blackberrying and
we always went over to the old farmhouse quite a lot. It's a
shame that was allowed to fall apart. Have you seen what
they've done at Beluncle – to the sheds in Jacobs's lane? We
always called it round the sheds because it's where the
Hangars were. That house down the bottom is the most
awful eyesore you ever saw – that was 2 farm cottages. I
don't like it – it's so ugly.

Everything changes.